Savoring the
Camino de Santiago

Savoring the Camino de Santiago

It's the Pilgrimage, Not the Hike

JULIE GIANELLONI CONNOR

Bayou City Press
THE WORLD IN PRINT

Bayou City Press, LLC
Houston, TX, USA
BayouCityPress.com
JulieConnorAuthor.com

Books may be purchased by contacting the publisher directly:
Bayou City Press, LLC, 10303 Scofield Lane, Houston, TX 77096
or by ordering from the publisher's website, BayouCityPress.com

Editing by Bayou City Press, LLC
Interior design by Eric Olson
Cover design by CoverKitchen
Map Illustrations by Mary Connor

978-1-951-331-03-0 (hardcover)
978-1-951-331-01-6 (paperback)
978-1-951-331-00-9 (ebook)
978-1-951-331-02-3 (audiobook)
Library of Congress Control Number: 2019954193

Publisher's Cataloging-In-Publication Data
(Prepared by The Donohue Group, Inc.)

Names: Connor, Julie Gianelloni, author.
Title: Savoring the Camino de Santiago : it's the pilgrimage, not the hike / Julie Gianelloni Connor.
Description: First edition. | Houston, TX, USA : Bayou City Press, LLC, [2019] | Includes bibliographical references and index.
Identifiers: ISBN 9781951331016 (paperback) | ISBN 9781951331009 (ebook)
Subjects: LCSH: Connor, Julie Gianelloni--Travel--Europe. | Camino de Santiago de Compostela--Description and travel. | Christian pilgrims and pilgrimages--Europe. | Spain--Description and travel. | LCGFT: Autobiographies. | Travel writing.
Classification: LCC BX2321.S3 C66 2019 (print) | LCC BX2321.S3 (ebook) | DDC 263.0424611--dc23

First Edition   Printed in the United States

THIS BOOK IS DEDICATED to all of my traveling companions over the years, but particularly to the three with whom I have traveled the most: my mother, Jeanette Catherine Singleton; my once-but-now-former husband, James E. Connor, Jr.; and my son, James A. Connor. My deceased mother and my former husband marched along with me in my thoughts for many, many miles on the Camino, and my son was the anchor I pulled behind me.

Contents

vii

CONTENTS CONTINUED

PREFACE

I WROTE PARTS OF THIS BOOK (the blog posts) while on the Camino, other parts once back home in Houston, and still other parts long after my journey. I don't think the Camino is something you should do quickly. It took me forty years before I finally made the pilgrimage, seven long weeks actually to walk the Camino's French route, and then three years of thinking about the pilgrimage before I finally finished this book.

Some chapters were presented to one of my critique groups, while others weren't. Sometimes feedback was very negative (Why would you ever do a trip like that? Who would ever want to read about it? It sounds horrible!). That negative reaction gave me pause. I wondered if my writing about the Camino was too negative, whereas I had striven to be balanced. Others liked the chapters I read, which encouraged me to continue.

It is hard to explain why I have continued with this goal of writing the book, when the fates seemed to conspire against it. Part of it is that I thought I could help others who were contemplating or planning a trip along the Camino. Part of it is that I had something to say. A large part of it is that no one else, among those I have read, delivered the message that I wanted to deliver and that I think is so important: you don't have to walk every step of the Camino, and you shouldn't put yourself in the mindset that you need to do so. Your goal should *not* be to walk every step, but rather to enjoy the Camino, to savor it, to wake up every day happy to continue your journey rather than dreading another slog down the road.

You will hear lots of people say things like "the Camino is whatever you want it to be," but mostly on the Camino you will hear disparaging remarks about others who are bicycling, or riding a bus, or (mortal sin) driving! Don't listen to those people. Respond by telling them about a great experience you had because you took the Camino at half-fast speed instead of running down the trail as quickly as you could.

The Camino is a pilgrimage, not just a long walk. My mother and sister went on a pilgrimage to Lourdes in 1955, my sister in a wheel chair. They walked very little, if at all. I can promise you that they, and the other pilgrims in their group, had a more authentic pilgrimage experience than many of the folks running along the Camino.

A pilgrimage is what you make of it, and what makes you feel spiritual, or religious, or connected to the universe. That comes to different people in different ways. For me, spending contemplative time in a magnificent church or a humble wayside chapel or stopping to observe the wildflowers along the way brings God closer to me and opens my mind to examining the state of my own spiritual and emotional health. I don't have that experience just walking steadily along as fast as I can. If walking does it for you, God go with you. If not, please don't allow yourself to feel that you have failed if you have decided to do a different kind of Camino. My advice: try to make every day as joyous as you can. If you find yourself wondering why you are not on a beach in southern Spain slurping down an umbrella drink, it's time to change up your travel plans. Find the joy.

Chapter 1
The Gun

IN THE AUTUMN OF 1971, I was the victim of violent crime. I was a junior at Rice University in Houston, Texas. On Sunday nights, dinner was not available in my assigned dining hall. One Sunday evening, I drove to a nearby restaurant. Outside, in the dark, under the spreading arms of an oak tree, a car pulled up beside me. In short order, a gun was pointed at me. I was forced at gunpoint to enter the other car, taken to a location quite a distance away, terrorized, knocked about, and sexually assaulted. I thought I was going to die. I was twenty years old, and I believed my life was over as I stared down the barrel of a loaded pistol.

I felt terror, true terror, the kind that, once you have experienced it, you realize is nothing akin to being scared or afraid. It is so fundamental that you are changed at your core. You realize that despite your everyday conviction that you are in control, that you make your own destiny, those beliefs are in fact rubbish. The events of that night, made possible by the gun, changed the path of my life, and eventually led me to the Camino de Santiago de Compostela (the Road to Santiago de Compostela). This book recounts my journey, and the things I learned along the Way.

Chapter 2
The Book

I FIRST HEARD ABOUT THE CAMINO DE SANTIAGO about
a year later. Following my encounter with the gun and the three
hoodlums behind it, I had dropped out of Rice University and
gone to live in Portugal in January 1972. I left college for a number of
reasons, one of them the gun, another financial worries. My parents
wanted me to come home to Baton Rouge, Louisiana, and go to
Louisiana State University (LSU), their alma mater. They said they
couldn't afford to keep me at Rice, but I knew they wanted me back
safe in Baton Rouge.

I had no desire to finish my degree at LSU. I had grown up loving
LSU, the alma mater of both my parents, but now my heart and my
history were anchored at Rice. If I finished my degree, which at that
time was not a sure thing, I wanted it to be at Rice. On the other
hand, I feared that those hoodlums might reappear in my life, perhaps to scare me away from testifying at trial after I identified them
to the police.

After my parents asked me to come home, at first I thought I
could finish at Rice by a combination of part-time jobs and student
loans. I had two jobs on campus, and I found a third off-campus job
as an au pair. But my heart wasn't in it. Everything seemed too hard.
I dropped out of Rice a week into the new semester, drove home, and
thought about what to do next.

The plan I came up with was to stay out of college for a year and work. After I had supported myself for a year, and had gotten off of my parents' income tax return, I could apply for financial aid at Rice under my own income, which would be basically zero. I could then finish out my last three semesters at Rice while amassing a lot less debt in student loans than if I had just continued on at Rice without a break.

At home in Baton Rouge after withdrawing from Rice, I decompressed from all of the stress and anxiety of the previous fall semester and tried to figure out what to do with the next year of my life. All during college, I had had jobs on campus. As a result, I had saved a bit of money. I wanted to use part of my savings to take a trip.

At that time, an older cousin of mine was teaching at West Point. I had visited him one long weekend my senior year in high school and had had a blast. I decided I would fly up and stay with him and his wife for a while. I told my mother that I was considering this. "If you are thinking of a trip," she said, "why not go to Europe instead?" I felt like I had been struck in the head with a hammer. My mother was suggesting I go to Europe? I was on board with that plan right away. West Point out, Europe in. And so began my foreign traveling life.

Fast forward nine months or so. In August 1972, I was living in a fifth-floor walk-up apartment in Lisbon, sharing it with a delightful New Zealand flatmate. Hilaire Kirkland was quite tall, almost six feet, with a sculpted face showing strong bone lines, and shoulder-length champagne-colored hair. She was a poet with a published booklet of poems. She was somewhat older than me, and had been knocking around the world and Portugal several years more than I had. She was a reader, too, and we frequently exchanged books and opinions on them.

"Here," she said, "you should read this book," handing me a copy of James Michener's *Iberia*. Like all of her books, Hilaire had carefully manufactured a homemade book cover with transparent, heavy plastic. Even now, when I reach for a certain older book from my shelves and see that it is covered in heavy plastic, I know that it was a gift from Hilaire.

I love travel books, and *Iberia* was the first travel book I fell in love with. I raced through *Iberia*, cover to cover. I read certain passages over and over. While Michener mainly writes about Spain, he covers Portugal somewhat too. I loved learning about the history of the Iberian Peninsula *a la* Michener and reading his depictions of the art and architecture in Spain. I loved his talk of food and restaurants and festivals. I plain fell in love with the book and wanted to follow in Michener's footsteps around Spain, visiting the places he talked about, eating at the restaurants he frequented, and meeting the Spaniards—from taxi drivers to countesses—to whom he had introduced me.

Unfortunately, I didn't have the resources to do that; I was living "on the economy" as a poorly paid teacher of English at a language school in Lisbon. But when I took small sips of Spain, on long weekends or over school holidays, I always re-read what Michener had to say about the place I was visiting.

When my future husband came over to Portugal to meet me, following his all-expenses-paid trip to Vietnam (a family military joke dating back at least to World War II), I recommended that he read Michener. Soon he was quoting chapter and verse of *Iberia* to me. "Yes, I *have* read the book," I would dryly reply. He quoted Michener so much that I began referring to it as "the Bible according to Michener."

In the last chapter of *Iberia*, Michener wrote about the Camino de Santiago. I had grown up on my mother's stories about her pilgrimage to Lourdes, to which she took my very ill sister, seeking a miraculous cure. In Portugal, I had had the opportunity to visit Fatima, in company with a priest (another story for another book). Going on a pilgrimage, or at least going to a pilgrimage town, was already part of my DNA before I read Michener. Raised as a Catholic, Lourdes and Fatima were in my religious geography, but it was

Michener who introduced me to Santiago de Compostela, one of the great pilgrimage sites since 812 AD.

Thanks to Michener, I had wanted to travel the Camino since 1972. Back in the early 1970s, however, I had neither the time nor the money to do so. Still, the Camino remained on my mind, something I wanted to do, when I could.

When I knew I was going, finally, to do the Camino pilgrimage, I started reading other travel books about the Camino. There are a lot of them out there. My favorite one is by an English author named Tim Moore who walked the Camino along with a donkey. Shirley MacLaine has written a famous account of her Camino trip. I have read about the trips of Germans and Americans and others. I recently learned about a Korean traveler who went home and wrote a best seller about his Camino trip. As a result, there are now a flood of Koreans following the yellow Camino arrow signposts. And since the movie *The Way* came out, hordes of American hikers have joined the river of pilgrims.

In 1985, I took a month-long trip to Spain with my mother and my cousin, Doris Julie Bracewell, whom I call D.J. Before that trip, I re-read all of Michener. *Iberia* was sadly dated in many ways. Michener had written many passages, and reported many conversations, on the future of Spain. Specifically, he reported discussions about what would happen to Spain when Spanish dictator Generalissimo Francisco Franco passed from the scene. When I first read *Iberia*, those passages were interesting, and relevant, not just for Spain, but also for Portugal, which was itself still living under the political regime established in the 1930s by dictator Antonio de Oliveira Salazar.

Would civil war break out in Spain, as it had in 1936? Or would Spain somehow manage a transition to democracy? It is hard now to image the tension such discussions caused. The Spanish Civil War was a brutal, murderous affair, every bit as, if not more, horrible as our own Civil War, with brother fighting against brother and horrific casualties. Moreover, the Spanish Civil War included a large measure of war against the civilian population. Sherman's March to Atlanta foreshadowed this type of "collateral damage," but in the intervening seventy-odd years military leaders had found new methods to intensify the atrocities inflicted on civilians.

Since I was living on the Iberian Peninsula, the issue of whether Spain would again devolve into civil war was therefore of great interest in 1972. By 1986, however, that question had been answered. Spain, amazingly, had moved peacefully to a constitutional monarchy under the leadership of its reinstated hereditary monarch, King Juan Carlos.

Other parts of *Iberia* also seemed dated when I re-read the book in 1986, such as Michener's mouth-watering depictions of certain restaurants. In 1986 I searched for some of the restaurants he mentioned, but came up empty. Either they had closed, or they were so obscure that hotel concierges had never heard of them. Nevertheless, many parts of *Iberia* remained relevant.

As I neared my latest trip to Spain, I thought about taking *Iberia* along with me. My son had bought me a Kindle for a Christmas gift. I admit that I had resisted moving into the digital book era. I love the feel of holding a book, the smell of a newly purchased volume, the security of having a title on my shelf for easy reference. But having a Kindle, and knowing that my son would be disappointed if I spurned this expensive-for-him gift, I started giving digital books a try. And I found all the obvious advantages of such digital books, particularly the advantage of taking the Kindle on trips in lieu of multiple heavy, hard-back books. I determined to load Michener on my Kindle rather than take the hard copy. In the meanwhile, I could pull my well-worn copy of Michener off my shelf and read the relevant chapter before my trip. The best of both worlds!

I went to my bookshelf to find my copy of *Iberia*. Uh-oh. Where is Michener? He is not where he is supposed to be, on my shelf in modern American literature. I was still getting my house in order, after having retired back to Houston in 2014. Maybe I placed him with my travel books in the front room? No, not there either. Do I still have an unopened box of books wrongly left in the storage closet with my old files? Not there either. After diligent searching, I had to admit the truth. My well-worn, plastic-covered, much-loved copy of *Iberia* was gone. I had lost a talisman, given to me by my dear departed Hilaire, a book inscribed with my name and the date I first read it.

What happened to my *Iberia*? With so many moves over the years, it was hard to tell. The last time I truly remembered consulting Michener was for that 1986 trip to Spain with my mother and my cousin. Maybe my copy was relinquished to my ex-husband at the time of the great book divide. After all, for me it was a wonderful travel book, but for him it was The Bible. Or maybe it had just gotten lost by packers. One thing for sure: I had not casually given it away.

I mourned the loss of this beloved tome for a couple of weeks. And then I resolved to move on. After all, I had the Kindle copy, right? Another week went by. It just didn't feel right. I passed a large bookstore at least twice, and each time I felt the magnetic pull of the bookstore and *Iberia*—but I resisted. I didn't really need two copies, one digital and one hard, did I? Still, *Iberia* niggled at the back of my brain. Since I was making multiple visits to a local sports store to gear up for my upcoming trip to Spain, and since the sports store sits in the same plaza as the bookstore, I couldn't get the idea of having a hard copy out of my head. Kindle is all well and good, but I needed a hard copy. On my bookshelf. Ready to move into my hand at any moment.

I finally gave in and went to the bookstore. I roamed the fiction bookshelves, finding the "M's" and then books by Michener. I found lots of copies of his other titles, most of which I have read, but I couldn't find *Iberia*. OK, the book *is* dated. Maybe nobody reads it anymore. I went to Customer Service, told the clerk that I had looked for it on the shelves but couldn't find it, and said that I would like to order a copy. The kindly looking male clerk checked his computer and said, "We have a copy."

"You do? I looked but couldn't find one. I saw *Hawaii* and *Poland* and *The Covenant*, but not *Iberia*. Could you perhaps help me find it?" At this point, I was feeling faintly smug. I had searched that bookshelf thoroughly. *Iberia* wasn't there. Nor was it misfiled anywhere nearby. I had checked adjoining shelves too.

"Certainly. Please follow me." The clerk led me to the travel section. I wanted to smack my head. Duh! Of course. *Iberia* is not fiction. It is a travel book. And there it was, nestled among other worthy travel guides. I grabbed my prized (new) copy and headed for checkout. At home, I turned to Chapter XIII, "Santiago de Compostela." Like always when I read *Iberia*, I absorb something new. This time, I learned that the Camino inspired the very first guidebook, written by a monk in 1130 AD.

I had been openly talking about going on the Camino for the last couple of years. I had originally been planning to make this my first post-retirement long trip. Walking the Camino would be a good way to figure out how I would spend the rest of my life. But fate, in the form of cancer, intervened. I postponed. And then postponed again.

One new Houston acquaintance of mine, to whom I had recounted my Camino hopes, invited me to a meeting of the West University Rotary Club, where Sally McCandless spoke about her Camino trip. Sally, who probably has a good ten years on me, started out by saying that she had been thinking about taking this walk for about twenty years. "Hah!" I thought. "I've got her beat. I've been wanting to do this for over forty years."

Another new friend told me about an organization that I had not heard of before, American Pilgrims on the Camino (APOC). APOC is a community of people who dispense advice to future Camino travelers and share Camino stories. The Houston chapter has regular gatherings, where I had the opportunity to ask veteran Camino pilgrims about everything from recommended boots to whether walking sticks were truly needed.

From APOC, I also learned about aspects of the trip that I didn't know, like that pilgrims at the end of their trip can get a "Compostela," a certificate verifying that the pilgrim has walked at least a hundred kilometers along the Camino. Michener never talked about the Compostela, which is issued by representatives of the Catholic Church in Santiago, so I doubted that he had received one. After learning about the Compostela, I immediately wanted one. What a great addition it would make to my travel memorabilia! I learned that when requesting the Compostela, pilgrims are asked whether they undertook the journey for religious, cultural, or health reasons. I planned to answer, "All three."

Chapter 3
The Big "C"

THE THIRD FACTOR PUSHING ME to undertake a pilgrimage to Santiago de Compostela was a diagnosis of breast cancer in January 2014.

In December 2012 I had my annual mammogram and got a clean bill of health. Once, around 1990, doctors had detected a lump and recommended a needle aspiration biopsy. I did that, and the result was negative. I have always had fibrous, "lumpy" breasts, so I did not really ever follow the recommendation to do a breast self-examination every month. When I did a self-examination, I always felt lumps, and, unless I was going to scare myself every month, doing the examination just wasn't going to be productive. I was, however, very strict with myself about getting an annual mammogram, even though the requirements of my career meant that I was having to find a new doctor every other year and carry around the world with me those large, old films that were state-of-the art before digital.

The December 2012 diagnosis of "no problem" was what I had expected. What I did not expect was that by the late fall of 2013 I would know something was wrong. I was having a throbbing in my left breast, and at times I felt a hot spot. Finally, I did a breast self-examination, and there was clearly a lump at the spot that throbbed and felt hot. I immediately phoned to make the appointment for my annual mammogram. I told the receptionist that I believed I had a lump. I tried to move up my appointment, but the schedule was full.

After my mammogram, I was surprised that I didn't get an immediate diagnosis of breast cancer. I was called in for more tests, then yet more tests. Finally, my gynecologist's office confirmed—I had breast cancer and needed to see an oncologist.

The oncologist asked for more tests. She explained that the results would dictate what treatment plan I would have. Different types of cancer respond to different treatments. The testing went on and on. I knew by December that I had cancer, yet treatment didn't start until March. Three months of no treatment, while the cancer was growing. My oncologist kept telling me not to worry—there was no evidence that the cancer had spread.

To tell the truth, I wasn't *too* worried. My mother had had breast cancer twice, with more than ten years between the two episodes, and she lived to be ninety. I knew that recovery rates had improved further since my mother's illness, so I knew that the odds were in my favor. Still, you can't help but worry.

And I had a lot of other pressures. I was working, but winding up my career. I planned to retire later that year and move to my permanent retirement location—which I had to pick. Retirement and moving are two of life's most stressful events, but piling cancer on top really was too much.

My Austin oncologist started me on the treatment plan she said had the best results for patients with my profile—chemotherapy, lumpectomy, and then radiation. I started the chemo while I was still working. I was renting a house in Austin, and I tried to extend my lease for a year, or six months, or even three months, so as to allow me to space out working, finishing chemo, packing up, and moving. But my landlord, even though he knew my circumstances, refused me extra time in the house, so I was going to have to move, either to another place in Austin or to my new retirement home, before finishing chemo. After so many moves over the course of my Foreign Service career, I wanted to move just one more time in my life. Half-way through chemo, I packed up and moved from Austin to Houston, finishing my chemo treatment at M.D. Anderson.

Of course, nothing is ever as expected. With a clean mammogram a year before, by the time I was diagnosed I was already at Stage 2. Still, oncologists both in Austin and Houston said there was no evidence the cancer had spread. My initial impulse, to have a full mastectomy rather than a lumpectomy, was checked by this good news. I went with the doctors' recommendation for a lumpectomy rather than a mastectomy. Waking up after surgery, I immediately knew that more had been done than anticipated. It turned out some lymph nodes had had cancerous cells, so all the lymph nodes on my left side were removed as well. I still had two months of radiation after that.

All of 2014 was a miasma of cancer. I survived, and my prognosis was good, but I now had neuropathy—numbness—in my fingers and toes from the chemotherapy, and lymphedema—swelling in my arm—from having my lymph nodes removed. My body seemed to be falling apart.

I had now had my second near-death experience.

Chapter 4
Putting It All Together

I FIRST HEARD ABOUT THE CAMINO over forty years ago. In 1971, just before dropping out of Rice, I was a victim of violent crime. One night, I thought my life was over. I expected to be shot at any moment. I felt terror, true terror, and came to realize that, in my hubris, I had thought I was in control of my life, but I never had been. Thanks to the powers that be, whether God or Jesus or St. James or pure fate, I had been granted another 44 years to live and travel.

Then, once again in 2014, I saw death, this time in the form of cancer, staring me in the face. I made it through chemotherapy, and surgery, and radiation, but my overall health was compromised, and there were no guarantees about the future. I knew that if I was ever going to go to Santiago, I needed to do it soon.

I decided. No more delays or postponements, no matter how important or worthy the reason to put off the trip. It was time to give thanks for cheating death twice, by going on pilgrimage to Santiago.

Chapter 5
The Camino: A Primer

IF YOU ALREADY KNOW A LOT about the Camino, which is also called "The Way of Saint James" in English, or if you have already read a book or two about it, you can feel free to skip this chapter or just to skim it. Most books on the Camino cover at least some of this same basic information.

Most cognoscenti just call it "the Camino," which is Spanish for "the path" or "the way" or "the road."

Those who walk the Camino are generally referred to as pilgrims (*peregrinos*, in Spanish), those who bike it are called *bicigrinos* (bicycle pilgrims), and those who drive the route are usually not thought of as pilgrims at all, but rather as tourists. (See Chapter 19, "Modern-Day Camino Myths and Prejudices," on page 96.)

Strictly speaking, there is no single "Camino." There are, rather, thousands of them. Each individual's route is his or her own Camino. There is, however, a fixed end point—the cathedral in the Spanish city of Santiago de Compostela, usually just referred to as Santiago. ("Santiago de Compostela" means "St. James of Compostela." More about "Compostela" is below.)

Originally, a pilgrim would step outside of his home and begin his pilgrimage, his Camino. This is still true today, with pilgrimages beginning from all over the world. I met one pilgrim who took this belief literally and walked out her front door to begin her pilgrimage. She said that it took her five days of walking just to reach LAX airport from her home, and she was surprised to find that most pilgrims only begin their pilgrimage after arriving at one of the traditional jumping off or gathering spots.

In the Middle Ages—and even today—it can be dangerous to walk the Camino. (Spanish authorities will tell you that the Camino is overwhelmingly safe, and in general it is. But at least one murder has occurred on the Camino in recent years.) Hence, in former times, it was traditional for pilgrims to gather in selected towns and begin their pilgrimage as a group—safety in numbers being the idea. Paris was one of the main starting points, though there were many others.

CAMINO ROUTES

Today the "French route" is the most traveled route, and this book focuses on that route. In the Middle Ages, many pilgrims started their journey in Paris, but many others gathered together in other French towns. In any event, the various French tracks join together at Saint-Jean-Pied-de-Port, a town on the French side of the Pyrenees. Saint-Jean-Pied-de-Port is usually referred to just as "St. Jean," and in writing you will frequently see it as "SJPP." A rough translation from the French would be "St. John at the Foot of the Mountain Pass."

From SJPP, pilgrims have two choices: either take the "high" route, which was used by Napoleon's soldiers when they crossed the Pyrenees, or the "low" route, which sounds good but still is daunting. Those who are fit, young, or pilgrimage fundamentalists; who want "the full experience"; or who are deluding themselves opt for the Napoleonic high route. The remainder, myself included, are grateful that there is a less strenuous option. Particularly so early in the journey, the last thing I wanted to do was to hurt myself, get lost in the mountains at night, or have any of the other myriad disasters that can and do happen to pilgrims happen to me.

The high and low routes both join up again, once the pilgrim is across the mountains and in Spain, at the town of Roncesvalles, which is the site immortalized in the epic French poem *The Song of*

Roland. Roncesvalles was the place where the famous French knight Roland, the favorite of Charlemagne, was betrayed and killed. The French route then wends its way across northern Spain, ending at Santiago de Compostela, which is inland but located not far from the western (Atlantic) coast of Spain. From Saint-Jean-Pied-de-Port to Santiago is about 500 miles along a marked trail.

The second most popular route nowadays is the Portuguese route, which can start in Lisbon or Oporto and then heads north towards Santiago. Other popular routes include the *Primitivo*, or "Primitive" route; the English route; the coastal route; and the various routes that start in the south of Spain. True Camino enthusiasts walk one route, then come back another year to walk another route.

Given the length of the routes and the shortness of vacations, some pilgrims break up the French route into segments (generally referred to as a "*stage*" while on the Camino), walking one segment one year, then returning the following year to walk another *stage*. For example, those with only a couple of weeks of free time might walk from Saint-Jean-Pied-de-Port to Burgos one year, then the next year Burgos to León, etc.

When planning a walking trip, it helps to figure out how fast you walk. Taking a few practice hikes while you are in the planning stages is highly recommended. First, it will help you break in your new boots and make sure you have bought the right ones. Among the most common abandoned objects along the Camino are hiking boots and tennis shoes—proof that footwear that felt fine in the store or for a stroll around a park can't stand up to the rigors of the Camino. But besides trying out your footwear, those practice hikes will give you a chance to time yourself. How long does it take you to walk a mile? Add in bathroom breaks, rest stops, water breaks, lunch, and so forth, and then figure out how far you can realistically walk in a day. And remember that you will be doing the same amount of walking every day, day after day. In general, I seemed to do about six hours of actual walking per day. Once I added a morning and afternoon drink and rest stop plus lunch, my daily Camino trek easily lasted from early morning until well into the afternoon.

SCHEDULING YOUR CAMINO

Like those who scuba dive, pilgrims on the Camino tend to be early birds. There are a number of reasons for this. First, for those bunking in hostels, the hostels fill up on a first-come, first-served basis, so you have to get to your next stop early enough to snare a bunk. Second, most pilgrims walk in summer, and it can get brutally hot in the afternoon—so if you can get most of your walking done early in the day, you can eat a leisurely lunch during the hottest part of the afternoon and then finish your walk once it cools off a bit.

For myself, I built into my schedule a rest day every week. I needed rest days for all sorts of activities, in addition to resting, such as washing clothes or finding a store to buy or replace clothes and equipment.

I also built into my schedule an extra day in the big cities—Burgos, León, Santiago. Each of those cities has magnificent cathedrals, museums, palaces, and other places I wanted to visit.

I never really understood those pilgrims I observed practically running down the Camino. They would brag about how far they had gone in a day. Or how quickly they planned to walk the whole *Camino Francais* (French route). They never stopped to duck into an open church in a small village, visit a museum, read a book under a tree, or chat with another pilgrim. "What's the point?" I would wonder.

You'll hear a lot of trite expressions along the Camino, one of which is, "It's not the destination; it's the journey." That saying is one with which I wholeheartedly agree. If all you desire is bragging rights about how fast you walked the Camino, then go ahead. Otherwise, if you have limited time, break your journey up into segments over a couple of years so that you can truly enjoy the experience, or at least can go home having seen something besides the actual trail under your feet.

HISTORY OF THE CAMINO

Depending on whether you are Catholic or Protestant, St. James was either a cousin of Jesus (Catholics) or his brother (Protestants). In any case, St. James was loved by Jesus, and, along with his brother John, James became one of Jesus's earliest disciples. James accompanied Jesus throughout his ministry, and was there at the time of the crucifixion.

After the death of Jesus, the apostles split up and went to proselytize in various countries. James wound up in Spain. Church history tells us that he was spectacularly unsuccessful in converting anyone to Christianity. He got terribly discouraged more than once. The Virgin Mary supposedly miraculously appeared to him a couple of times, giving him encouragement and the will to continue.

Eventually James was successful in converting a few Spaniards. After some years, he decided to return to Palestine and was accompanied by at least a couple of those he had converted. Upon reaching Palestine, James was almost immediately arrested by King Herod Agrippa. He was beheaded in 44 AD. He was the first of the apostles to be martyred. Two of his converts then took his body back to Spain for burial, supposedly transporting the body on a "stone boat." James was buried in Spain, and over time the memory of that burial site was lost.

Fast forward to the year 812 (or maybe it was 814) AD. A hermit observed a bright star where one had never been before. (Sound familiar?) He went to investigate and found a couple of graves, one marked as being that of James, and the other bearing the name of one of James's converts. The local Catholic bishop was called in, and the bishop quickly certified that the grave indeed was that of St. James. Before long, a church, the first of several, was built on the spot, the "Field of the Star," or *campo de la estrella* in Spanish. This is the most common explanation for the derivation of the place name "Compostela," but, like many of the facts about the history of Santiago, there are those who prefer alternate explanations. To those other groups, "Compostela" comes from the Latin, either "campus stellae" (field where the star shown) or "compost terra" (burial ground). In any case, before too long, this place came to be known as Santiago de Compostela.

As for the name "James," in Spanish as in English it has many variants. Whereas out of James we make "Jim" or "Jimmy" or "Jamie," the Spanish have "Jaime" and "Diego." Hence Saint (San) James (Diego) becomes, over time, Santiago. Over the years and on the Camino, James was also referred to by many other variations: Jacobus, Iago, Jacome, Jacques.

THE PILGRIMAGES BEGIN

Almost immediately following the discovery of James's grave in 812 AD, devout Christians began to flock to the site. Before very long, making a pilgrimage to Santiago became one of the "big three" possible pilgrimages, with the other two being pilgrimages to Jerusalem or Rome. By the 1100s, a vast multitude of Europeans—estimated as being between 500,000 and two million annually—were making their way to Santiago.

Among these pilgrims were numerous kings, such as Charlemagne (Holy Roman Empire), Alfonso II (Spain), and Louis VII (France). Some judges in the Middle Ages ordered convicted criminals to undertake pilgrimages in lieu of jail time, and some priests decreed that certain sinners walk the Camino as penance. Kings, saints (St. Francis of Assisi), and rich people rubbed shoulders along the way with thieves, murderers, and other brigands. In more recent times, famous folk as varied at Pope John XXIII and Shirley MacLaine have made pilgrimages to Santiago.

Given the lack of fast transport in the Middle Ages, the decision to walk to Santiago, or even to ride a horse or mule there, was a major undertaking. Pilgrims might be gone for a couple of years on the journey, and due to the ardors of the trip might never make it home again. Despite those difficulties, the river of humanity continued flowing to Santiago for hundreds of years.

All along the route, the Catholic Church constructed monasteries, "hospitals," and other facilities to feed, shelter, and take care of the faithful. Many saints achieved sainthood by humbly serving the needs of the pilgrims, and many of the most popular medieval saints were beloved because of their selfless service to all those pilgrims.

The Knights Templar, in particular the Spanish branch whose symbol was a red cross, took as their mission the protection of the pilgrims. One of the more interesting stops along the French route is a town boasting a beautifully preserved castle built by the Knights Templar.

Pilgrims to Santiago traditionally wore a voluminous heavy cloak to shield them from the elements. A broad-brimmed hat, usually pinned up in the front, shaded them from the fierce Spanish sun. Stout sandals protected their feet from the rocky, hard-baked soil. And each pilgrim carried a thick, eight-foot-long walking stick topped by a crook, like the staffs that shepherds use, with a gourd affixed to the crook. The walking stick offered balance down slippery, treacherous slopes and served as a cudgel against attacking dogs, wolves, or villains, each category of which were numerous along the Camino. The gourd was the canteen of its time.

Over the course of a journey, a pilgrim to Santiago would usually wear out several pairs of sandals. Today's pilgrims, who see discarded hiking boots and sneakers all along the Camino, are only seeing what their medieval counterparts would also have seen—lots of footwear that didn't survive the trip.

On his return journey, the pilgrim sported an additional item— a cockleshell from the Spanish coast. Over time, the cockleshell became the symbol of those traveling the Camino, and pilgrims wore them proudly.

St. James Disappears (Again)

The bones of St. James were lost for a second time, following Sir Francis Drake's attack on the Spanish port city of Coruña in 1589. The sitting bishop of the time ordered the saint's bones be hidden in order to protect them, and the bones stayed hidden until 1879 when they were rediscovered and then ratified as being authentic by the Pope.

During those almost three hundred "lost" years, the number of pilgrims to Santiago naturally decreased dramatically. And of course, the faith of the Middle Ages had been replaced by scientific and rational thinking. Over the "lost" centuries and then during the decades following the rediscovery, the number of pilgrims to Santiago dried up to the merest trickle of persons on an annual basis, in contrast to the huge river of humanity that had flowed to Santiago from the 9th century until 1589. The once prosperous towns all along the pilgrimage route fell on hard times. By the 1950s, many of those towns were practically ghost towns.

In modern Catholicism, pilgrimages in general are not nearly as popular as they were during the Middle Ages. And when they do occur, such pilgrimages usually have as a destination a site associated with the Virgin Mary. For example, some of the faithful still go to Lourdes or Fatima to seek the intercession of the Virgin Mary for some health problem or other issue. Throughout Latin America, there are traditions of walking to holy sites, or sometimes even going to holy sites on one's knees, usually in fulfillment of a vow. For example, "If you save my sick child, I will go to a holy place in gratitude." Every year, around holy days in many predominantly Catholic countries, one can observe a procession of such worshippers as they make their journeys to holy sites. Such pilgrimages, however, usually last a day, or maybe a few days—seldom as long as a week. In short, the extended pilgrimages of the Middle Ages just aren't a feature of the modern Christian world.

THE CAMINO REVIVAL

Enter an incredible priest, Father Elías Valiña. A scholarly man, Father Elías (as he is known) had studied the history of the Camino. In the early 1970s, Father Elías got himself appointed as the priest at the parish church in O'Cebreiro, one of the more famous pilgrim towns along the route. Armed with a Ph.D. on the subject of the Camino, Father Elías went around Europe, attending conferences at which he read papers on the Camino. He also would travel around the Spanish countryside, painting yellow arrows on trees and fences. The yellow arrows all pointed in the direction of Santiago.

Father Elías's promotion of the history and routing of the Camino gave rise to increased interest in the Camino. That interest has continued to increase since the 1970s, spurred by a number of factors, including the movie *The Way*. Nowadays, as many as 300,000 individuals from all over the world make the pilgrimage to Santiago each year—on foot, bike, horseback, or via cars or buses.

Many pilgrims undertake the trip not for religious reasons, but because the Camino has become a famous walking adventure, Europe's equivalent of the Appalachian Trail or the Pacific Coast Trail. Moreover, the Camino has once again become an international highway, with the pilgrim sitting next to you at a local café in a tiny village as likely to be from Korea as from France. Biking the Camino has also become tremendously popular, and every day along the Camino you will see and hear packs of bicyclists in their tight spandex shouting to each other in Italian and French as they whiz past you.

Ye Shall Know Them by Their Signs

The modern-day symbols of the pilgrim include not only the cockleshell, but also the gourd and the yellow arrow. Almost all pilgrims have a cockleshell secured somewhere about their person, with having it affixed to one's backpack probably the most popular way to declare oneself a *peregrino*. Many pilgrims also carry a gourd attached to a walking staff or backpack. And at most crossroads along the Camino, with a quick look around, the pilgrim will see a yellow arrow pointing the way to Santiago. Given how poorly Spanish roads are sometimes marked, and given the off-the-paved-road path the Camino frequently takes, finding a yellow arrow when confronted with three divergent dirt cow paths generally elicits a sigh of relief.

Those yellow arrows lead pilgrims, like a real life "yellow brick road," to the emerald city of Santiago, where the cathedral built over the tomb of St. James still awaits pilgrims, as it has since the first iteration of the church went up in the 9th century. Once having done the Camino, any sighting of a cockleshell, or a gourd, or a yellow arrow will immediately bring the Camino to mind. Once you start seeing the cockleshell, you see it everywhere.

Chapter 6
To Walk (the Whole Way) or *Not* To Walk It—That Is the Question!

I DON'T KNOW HOW I BECAME SEDUCED by the idea of walking the Camino. For over forty years I had wanted to travel the Camino, ever since reading Chapter XIII of James Michener's *Iberia*, which is devoted to the Camino. Published in 1968, the book is based on Michener's travels throughout Spain. One thing is sure—Michener did not walk the Camino. At that time, almost no one did. Michener was driven along the Camino by knowledgeable friends who guided him, arranging meetings and meals with local experts. The Camino sounded fascinating, and after reading that chapter I wanted to follow the pilgrims' route.

Back then, when I first read Michener, I was in my early 20s, teaching English as a Foreign Language (TEFL) in Lisbon, Portugal. I was making a very small salary, enough to support my living on the local, then very inexpensive, Portuguese economy, but with very little money to spare. In whatever free time I had, I traveled around southern Europe. Sometimes I hitchhiked with a friend. Sometimes I took a train or a special inexpensive airplane charter for students. What I never did was hike. And what I did not have was either the time or the money to travel the whole length of the Camino. But my interest never waned.

Forty plus years later, the whole situation had changed. With retirement looming, I began to plan my future jaunts. I wanted to do at least one long trip per year. I picked the Camino as my first long trip.

Besides the changes in my own circumstances, the situation of the Camino had itself vastly changed since Michener's time. Due to the incredible efforts of Father Elías Valiña, interest in the Camino exploded starting in the 1990s. In 1986, fewer than 2,500 people obtained their Compostela, which is a document verifying that a pilgrim has walked at least the last 100 kilometers of the Camino. In 2018, more than 320,000 people obtained their Compostela.

Many additional pilgrims walk only portions of the Camino along one of the many different routes available, without qualifying to obtain a Compostela. Still others, particularly return pilgrims who already have a Compostela from a previous trip, don't bother applying for an additional one. The actual number of walkers in 2015, then, was actually well above the official figure of 260,000 pilgrims. Nowadays it seems almost everyone chooses to walk (rather than drive, for example) the Camino, as did most, but not all, pilgrims in medieval times. The culture of the Camino is predominately a walking culture.

When I began to think about scheduling my Camino trip, I began reading relevant books. Almost all of them recount the trips of walking pilgrims. Moreover, the recent pilgrims I met through APOC were all walkers. Gradually, as I read and listened to other pilgrims, the idea of walking the whole Camino dripped slowly and relentlessly into my brain.

Now, having walked the Camino, I want to offer an alternate vision. I advise those thinking about the Camino to consider carefully before deciding to walk, particularly before deciding to walk the whole French route, which stretches from Saint-Jean-Pied-de-Port in France through the Pyrenees into Spain, and then through northern Spain to Santiago de Compostela, where St. James the Apostle is buried.

Please don't misunderstand. I strongly urge you to travel the Camino, but you don't, and I believe shouldn't, plan to walk the whole way unless you can meet a series of tests.

Test 1. Do you love to walk? Do you get up in the morning and plan your daily perambulation? Do you faithfully do your daily walk? If you don't get to do your walk by bedtime, do you feel that something is missing from your day? You will be doing an awful lot of walking on the Camino, and if you don't naturally like walking, you will begin to regard it as a chore, not a delight. If your answer to these questions is "yes," then you are a good candidate to consider walking the Camino.

Test 2. When you walk, do you walk long distances, such as ten miles for several straight days? On the Camino, most people walk at least 25 kilometers per day, which is 15.5 miles. And they do that day after day. Even if you walk that much every day, with no rest days, it will take you more than four weeks to reach Santiago. If your answer to this question is also "yes," then you are an excellent candidate to walk the Camino.

Test 3. When you walk, do you go up and down hills and mountains? Or, if you live in a flat part of the world, do you go out of your way to climb stairs instead of taking elevators and regularly go to stadiums and climb the steps? The Camino goes through mountains at both ends, and substantial hills are found throughout. Except for the region called the Meseta, there are no "flat" regions on the Camino. The locals will tell you that the next day's trail is "easy," but don't be fooled. If you live in a mountainous or hilly area, and love walking up and down inclines, walking the Camino is definitely for you. If you are a flatlander, think very carefully. Spend a week going to the top of a stadium ten times every day. Does this feel like something you would enjoy doing day after day? If your answer is "yes," you are just the right person to walk the Camino.

Test 4. Are your feet, knees, and hips in good shape? Walking the Camino is brutal on all of these. As I walked along the Camino, I can't tell you how many other walkers passed me wearing knee braces. If you are confident that all of your parts can hold up to a rugged trial, walking the Camino is for you.

Test 5. Are you a sure-footed individual? The Camino is not well maintained in many sections. There are often slippery downhill slopes. At least two sections that I walked—the last portion into Zubiri and the final descent into Portomarin—were truly dangerous. If you are confident that you are part mountain goat (and hiking sticks help with this confidence), by all means tackle walking the Camino.

Test 6. Can you afford to buy the equipment you need, and can you afford to replace your equipment if it turns out not to be right or to wear out? One of the most common sights along the Camino is abandoned hiking shoes and boots. Buying the right hiking boots can be expensive, and if you don't get the right ones you are going to have to replace them. If you can afford to buy new boots, replace your hiking poles if they break, spring for that fleece-lined jacket you didn't think you would need, and pay for other unexpected expenses, walking the Camino could be the right choice for you.

Test 7. Are you a very healthy person, not prone to colds, aches, pains, etc.? Are your knees in good shape? What about your feet? Walking the Camino is strenuous enough by itself. Having to do it when you don't feel well or ache will truly test your fortitude. There is a reason the books about the Camino are full of references to walkers popping ibuprofen 600 mg tablets four times a day. I personally saw very ill persons refuse to give up walking, which was a loony sort of obsession equivalent to anything Cervantes wrote about Don Quijote de la Mancha. If you remain healthy while people all around you are coming down with colds, backaches, and the like, the Camino could be your cup of tea.

Test 8. Have you ever dreamed of running a marathon, or walking the Appalachian Trail or the Pacific Coast Trail? The Camino is exactly that, a grueling, long-distance experience. If you are excited by the thought of testing your endurance, let the Camino be your testing ground.

Test 9. Are you stubborn? I can assure you that the following thoughts will come to you along the Camino: *Why am I doing this? Why am I putting myself through this torture when I could be relaxing on the beach drinking a delicious cocktail?* I haven't read one book about the Camino in which the writer doesn't admit questioning the wisdom of undertaking this walk. If you have a stubbornness in your nature that compels you to complete objectives you have set for yourself, the Camino can be a wonderful self-imposed challenge.

Test 10. Do you love the idea of walking the Camino to the exclusion of all else, or do you want to have time to visit cathedrals and churches, enjoy art and history museums, and explore side trails with interesting cultural sites? If you make the decision to walk the Camino, you will have little time or energy to do anything else. Walking will take up six to nine to twelve hours of your day. Your whole focus is on getting to the next stopping place as quickly as possible, not on stopping to savor the Camino. If it is the physical challenge that most appeals to you, rather than the history and culture of the Camino, walking the Camino is for you.

Test 11. Are you going with a companion? Do your companion's answers to these test questions mirror your own answers? I witnessed a lot of veiled unhappiness on the Camino when one partner was committed to walking the whole way but the other one wasn't. Avoid this sure path to partner unhappiness. I suggest revising your plan. Either walk by yourself, or have your partner join you for only part of the trip, or give your partner the guilt-free freedom to ride the bus or stay an extra day in a town and then catch up with you down the road.

If you answered "yes" to most of the eleven tests above, then I urge you to walk the whole Camino. It will be an experience unlike any other, and you may well join the cadre of people who return to the Camino again and again for its unique qualities.

But what if you answered "no" to some of the questions above? Then I urge you to reconsider your plan to walk the whole way. There are alternatives.

(1) Bicycle the Camino, if you like bicycling. Many people, particularly the Italians and French, do.

(2) Ride the Camino horseback. If you are prepared to be on horseback for eight hours a day, there are riding trips. A hotel manager I met told me that he had seen every form of transportation possible on the Camino, including a camel, except for an elephant—and he thought that one of those would probably come through eventually.

(3) If you like motorcycles, travel the Camino by motorcycle.

(4) Or, plan a mixed trip—sometimes walking, sometimes taking a bus or train, sometimes taking a taxi if no bus or train is available. This is what I did, and what I recommend you do, unless you are one of those hearty travelers who could answer "yes" to all or most of the tests I posed above.

(5) Drive the Camino. You'll do a lot of walking just by visiting the sites along the way. If you drive with a companion or friends, you will have the freedom to switch off the driving and walk a *stage* of the Camino once in a while, if you decide to do so.

Above all, I recommend remaining flexible. Do not tell all your friends and relatives that you are going to walk the whole Camino. Give yourself some wiggle room. Say you are going to walk as much of it as you can, or as much of it as your available time allows, or as much of it as your health permits. Don't commit yourself to walking all of it, only to find that you can't keep that commitment to yourself and are embarrassed to admit the truth.

I know that this all sounds like common sense, and you will wonder why I bother setting it out. I can tell you that a reverse snobbery has taken over the Camino, and you will feel it everywhere once you embark on this trip. Pilgrims will tell you that if you don't walk every step of the way, you are not a "true" pilgrim. They will tell you the same if you don't carry all of your belongings on your back. (There are alternatives to carrying everything yourself.) They will tell you that if you don't stay in pilgrims' hostels, listening to the snoring and smelling the nighttime odors of multiple people, you are not a "real" pilgrim. Don't listen to those false prophets. Don't let yourself be persuaded to be miserable on the Camino. James Michener, a true pilgrim in every cell of his body, did not walk the Camino, and you don't have to either.

Does this philosophy make me a modern-day Camino heretic? Without doubt, many will tell you so. My own opinion is that doing the pilgrimage in the way that most conforms to putting and keeping you in a positive, spiritual frame of mind is the best way, in fact the only way, the Camino should be undertaken. If taking a very long walk is what you really desire to do—consider the Appalachian or Pacific Coast trails as possible alternatives. On the other hand, if you want to do a pilgrimage rather than a long hike, walking the whole way is not necessarily the best choice.

Chapter 7
Gearing Up

BEFORE MY TRIP, I SPENT MONTHS asking, reading, and talking about gear for the Camino. I made regular forays to a local sports outfitter to check out what was available. I carefully weighed the pros and cons of different options. Here is what I learned, and what I recommend.

Hiking Boots. This is the most important equipment you will buy. Spend all the time you can to make sure you have the right ones. They should be, above all, comfortable. You should buy them big, so that you have room to wear two pairs of socks (see below) and still not have your toes feel squeezed. I have big, wide feet, and after a lot of research and consulting, I bought Keen's in a men's size. They never let me down. The sports store I used, REI, has a policy allowing the return of hiking boots, even after use, if it turns out that the boots don't work for you. That means you can buy the boots, use them on a hike or two, and make sure you have bought the right boots. This is a great incentive to buy your hiking boots there.

Regular Shoes or Sandals. After your daily walk, you will want to change your hiking boots for something lighter and cooler. I saw every kind of footwear imaginable while on the trail, including flip flops and open-toed sandals, but it's best to stick with your hiking boots while on the trail. I can't tell you how many times my hiking boots saved me from stubbed toes due to half-buried rocks even on seemingly "flat" stretches of the Camino. Then at night, I (and everybody else) would shed my boots and socks and slip into my most comfortable footwear. On the trail I saw lots of people wearing sports shoes with "cut-out" sides that offered lots of ventilation. I got myself a pair, and love them—but for relaxing and cooling off after the walk.

Socks. The Camino veterans I spoke with before the trip all recommended a pair of silk liners under good, heavy, wool socks. I was a bit skeptical. Wool in hot summertime Spain? But I trusted those I had consulted and went with the wool socks. It worked. My feet did get hot at times, but the heavy socks helped cut down on blisters, the No. 1 enemy along the Camino.

Shoe Laces. The ones that came with my Keen boots were too short. The long laces I bought to replace the short ones were very long (good in terms of the ease of tying them) but constantly came untied (bad). I would have to stop and retie my boots every hour or so. I finally was tying multiple loose knots in the laces, just to keep the laces from constantly untying themselves. This is one conundrum I never completely solved. When my son was a toddler, I bought him some contraptions that meant we didn't have to tie his laces at all. The contraptions, styled like red plastic airplanes, kept the laces taut. If I could have found something similar along the way, I would have put them on my boots.

Walking Poles. Of all the equipment recommended to me, I was most skeptical about the need for walking sticks. Were they really worth the expense and the bother of carrying? Now having walked the Camino, I can answer these questions: Yes, yes, yes. Do not leave home without your walking sticks. Other than my boots, these were the most valuable pieces of equipment I carried with me. Going up and down hills and mountains is slippery in itself. Add to this, much of the Camino is not as well maintained as it could be. Further, many slopes are strewn with shale, making the surface under your feet inherently unstable. I soon came to appreciate my walking poles, which effectively made me a four-legged, rather than two-legged, creature, and hence much more stable. Many, many days I offered thanks to my Camino mentor and other Camino veterans for having persuaded me that walking sticks were required gear on the Camino.

I spoke with one lady who told me that she had already fallen four times. I noted that she had no walking sticks with her, and strongly urged her to go buy some before she fell and hurt herself to the point that she would have to curtail her trip. As for myself, I didn't have even one fall, thanks to my walking sticks (and thanks to going slowly and carefully over slippery terrain).

By the way, I bought, and am glad I did, the telescoping kind of walking pole. That made it possible for me to pack my walking sticks in my checked luggage on international flights, and also allowed me to strap the walking sticks onto my daypack when I didn't need them. (At the sight of any slope, I unstrapped them and put them to use.) I believe that buying the telescoping kind was well worth the extra cost. I also invested in a "light weight" make, and that, too, was worth the cost. On the Camino, every extra ounce turns into additional pain.

Pants. My Camino mentor recommended cargo pants to me, and it was a fabulous suggestion. She told me that she kept her passport in one thigh pocket, easy to access. And in the other, she carried a map. I did the same, and it was wonderful to have easy access to those items and not have to put my daypack down and rummage for the map whenever I needed to consult it. I also carried a small guidebook in a pocket.

Along the Camino, you will see every sort of getup you can imagine—short shorts, leggings, capri pants, skirts. Since I am prone to sunburn, I stuck with lightweight long pants, and am glad I did.

Underwear. Sports outfitters and travel catalogues sell many brands of fast drying underwear for men and women. If you plan to be washing out your underwear yourself, those are probably a good investment. I just used my regular underwear, which worked fine for me. My son, however, wished that he had bought and used sports underwear that would have helped cut down on the chaffing that he experienced.

Backpack. You will need a small backpack that you can carry with you every day. Many, many people, including even the budget crowd staying at auberges, arrange to send their heavy luggage on ahead to their next night's lodging rather than to lug everything every step of the way. There are those who object to this "cheating" (see Chapter 19, "Modern-Day Camino Myths and Prejudices," on page 96), but most pilgrims sensibly prefer to spare their backs and feet and leave the schlepping to a professional company that will move the luggage ahead for a small fee. (Usually 5 euros per move, in 2016.) But, even having dispatched your heavier luggage ahead, you still need your "daypack."

I purposely bought a smaller-than-average backpack. I know that I have rat-pack tendencies and fill up all available carrying spaces. My solution was to buy a smallish daypack to prevent myself from carrying stuff I didn't really need. I did spend a bit more for a backpack whose look I liked (it happened to be an Osprey). Why travel every day with something that looks utilitarian and ugly? I made sure it had several pockets, to store stuff I wanted to be able to access easily, and rings from which I could attach carabiners.

My son went for a military-style backpack and daypack, with webbing that allowed him to attach a lot of items to the packs.

We were both satisfied with our choices for backpacks.

A big decision I had to make was whether to buy a hydration pack, which is a plastic insert for a backpack that allows the hiker to suck water through a plastic tube, obviating the need to carry plastic water bottles on the trail. I had seen hydration packs being used on an earlier trip, and it seemed like a better solution than carrying a water bottle. Once having decided to buy the hydration pack, I had to decide how big a one to use. I went with a two-liter model, and I never ran out of water. The real trick is that you have to remember to fill up the hydration pack before setting out each morning. It sounds stupid to say it, but believe me sometimes we forgot. In those cases, you can always purchase bottled water along the way. My son bought a hydration pack that had a pump, and he liked it.

Knife. I carried a Swiss knife but rarely used it. My son carried a knife and used it all the time. Be sure to pack your knives in your checked luggage. I purchased a souvenir letter opener and then packed it in my carry-on for the return journey, only to have it confiscated at the Spanish security checkpoint. Any "blade" of a certain length, even if it is totally dull and with a rounded tip and clearly designed to be a souvenir, needs to be placed in checked rather than carry-on luggage.

Credit Card. Be sure to take one with you, and make it one that does not charge foreign transaction fees. You will unexpectedly need to buy things along the way: new boots, when yours wear out or don't work out; a new hat, when you leave yours at the lunch stop; or a splurge at an expensive hotel, when all you want is to swim in a pool and be pampered with good towels and hot water.

By the way, there is no need to carry lots of money. ATMs are all over, and they will dispense Spanish money to you.

Poncho. I carried a very lightweight poncho in my daypack. As it turned out, we were incredibly lucky and I only had to use the poncho once—but walking is miserable enough (for me, at least) without also being wet and cold. On some days there was a misty sort of rain, and I didn't even bother to break out my poncho on those days. The mist kept the day cool and made walking more comfortable. On the one day when there was heavy rain, I was glad to have my poncho in my daypack.

Cell Phone. Having one, and being able to use it, is very important. But be careful to select the right options. I didn't, and we suffered for it. (See Chapter 9, "Mistakes," on page 45.) Cell phones have no problem being plugged into Spanish electricity, but you have to have the right adaptors.

Adaptors. Buy and take several. You'll use them to plug in and recharge your cell phone, tablet, etc. Spanish plugs have three round holes, straight across. Your adaptors need to have two or three round prongs, straight across.

Camino Maps. You'll need these. John Brierley's guidebooks contain good maps of the Camino. I carried along his bigger book (in my heavy luggage) and his small map book (in my cargo pants pocket). You can check the titles of these books in Chapter 28, "Reading and Resources Suggestions," on page 242.

Road Map. I also carried a map of Spanish roads. Sometimes, you want to know where the paved road (as opposed to the Camino) goes. You might want to take a bus one day, or take a bus part way. Having a road map allows you to see where to get off the bus to pick up the Camino. Or you may want to walk along the road rather than the Camino, because the road offers a shorter route. Or you may want to avoid a particularly difficult or poorly maintained stretch of the Camino. There are all sorts of reasons for needing a road map.

Elevation Map. One item I didn't have when I left home was an elevation map. However, the tourism office in Saint-Jean-Pied-de-Port had a double-sided single sheet elevation map that I used every day on the Camino. (I tucked it into my Brierley map book.) The map breaks the Camino into 33 *stages* and shows the elevation along each *stage*. Whether you like or dislike walking up and down hills and mountains, the elevation map lets you know what is ahead so that you can plan your walk for the day.

Belt. If you wear cargo pants, as I have suggested, and start putting items in your pockets, your pants will sag. I don't usually wear a belt, but I needed one on the Camino. At the store, I was leaning towards a leather belt, but my son strongly recommended a webbed belt (the kind the military use). That turned out to be a good choice.

Hat. Even if you don't normally use a hat, get and wear one. (See Chapter 8, "Aches and Pains," on page 38.) Make sure you use a wide-brimmed one that will keep the sun off your face and neck.

Tablet. I love books, and carried more of those than I should have. I also carried my tablet, on which I loaded a number of books that I knew I wouldn't be using every day as well as novels set in Spain. Most hostels and hotels in Spain have WiFi, so you can use your tablet to surf the Internet if you need to do so or want to check in with family and friends. There are also lots of WiFi stores where you can buy plugs, cords, etc. I used my tablet a lot, and was glad I had taken it with me. Of course, you can also get most things nowadays on your phone, but if you are planning to do a lot of reading or keep a journal or anything like that, a tablet is handy.

Chapter 8
Aches and Pains

NO ONE COMES BACK from the Camino unscathed. If you are especially lucky, your injuries will be minor and will not interfere with your trip. If you are just normal, something will happen to you on your walk that will mean you have to go for medical assistance. And if you are really unlucky, your injury will have a major impact on your pilgrimage, either curtailing it or changing its nature.

Before the trip, I talked with a lot of people about their experiences and did a lot of reading about the Camino. The most common complaint seemed to be that everyone who walks the Camino develops blisters. I prepared for blisters. I learned about how to drain them with a cauterized needle and thread, what the best blister pads were, and so forth. I prepared a special "blister pack" that I made sure to carry in my daypack whenever I walked. At lunchtime, my son and I would take off our boots and socks to give our feet a rest. We'd immediately treat any blisters or "hot spots" that had developed.

On our trip, I was the lucky one. Occasionally I had shoulder aches, caused by carrying too much weight on one side. I'd stop along the trail and shift around items in my daypack to move the weight from one side to the other side, or to move items out of my daypack and attach them to my waist, or to carry my daypack over just the non-aching shoulder for a while. These were just small pains.

Although it sounds ridiculous to say it, I was lucky in having continuing neuropathy in my toes due to chemotherapy. I got some minor blisters along the way, but, because I couldn't feel them, they didn't hurt. A silver lining.

The worst for me was that I came home with blackened toenails. Despite not hurting, they looked awful. At a visit to my podiatrist after I was home again, he said that two toenails were loose and would eventually come off—but they never did. I just had to be patient and wait for the toenails to grow out so that the blackened areas could gradually be snipped off. It was at least nine months before my toenails were in sufficiently good shape to allow me to apply nail polish.

I didn't really have any other physical ailments. I took a couple of ibuprofen a couple of times, and that was it.

My son was the unlucky one. He suffered from a multitude of problems. Early on, he caught a bad cold, and just wanted to sleep for several days. Having to get up each morning and move on was a misery for him. He had a persistently itchy scalp, until a pharmacist diagnosed it as a sunburned scalp causing dryness. (Thank goodness that is what it was. I had feared head lice!) My son has abundant hair, and despite living in tropical countries he had never before had a sunburned scalp. Perhaps the mountainous altitude was a factor. He solved this problem by using the right shampoo and consistently wearing a hat. He also had chaffing between his legs, which was very uncomfortable, and backaches. But the worst problem was his feet.

He had a much worse blister problem than I ever did. He would use up my blister pack supply, and we would stop and buy more. And then about a third of the way through our trip, my son began to complain that his foot—not his blisters, but his foot—was hurting him. My feet often hurt at the end of the day, too, but just in the normal way of feet being hot, cramped, and worn out after a long day of walking up and down mountains and hills. For me, taking a nap with my feet up solved the issue.

For my son, the hurt began early each day and didn't let up for the whole day. While I heard my son's complaints about his foot, I more or less ignored them. After all, he was young, healthy, and still walking. Maybe complaining about his feet was just his way of registering a protest.

I don't know any pilgrim who, at some point in his or her walk, doesn't say to himself, "Why the heck am I here? Why am I *doing* this to myself? I could be lying on the beach at Marbella, or lounging in a café in Madrid. What was I thinking! This is crazy!" When you have been walking for hours; are hot, tired, and hungry; surmount what you think is your last mountain before your daily destination, only to see yet another mountain in front of you—insidious thoughts then start going around and around in your head. You can't help it. You resolve to quit the walk at the next town and take a bus/train/plane out of northern Spain for a more comfortable destination. I knew I was having these thoughts, so I just assumed complaining about his feet was my son's way of saying he was fed up without actually saying it. I ignored him.

Along about Day 7 of the complaining, we met up with a pilgrim that we knew and settled down to lunch with her. A male friend of hers also joined us. Inevitably, the talk turned to aches and pains. The guy told us that he had already been to the emergency room *five times*, usually to get some help for his blisters. I was quietly flabbergasted. This was a seemingly healthy man, big and strong. Five times to the emergency room? His feet must be an incredible mess. How was he still walking?

Our other lunch companion mentioned that she, too, had made a trip to a clinic, also for foot problems.

I resolved then and there to take my son to a clinic. At the first opportunity, we asked where we could get primary care and immediately went there. The doctor, a woman of middle years who first saw us, when hearing that my son had a foot problem, immediately said, "Bad blisters?"

"No," I replied. "It's something else. His foot is just always hurting."

Off we went with the doctor to an examination cubicle. The doctor ticked off items as she looked at my son's feet. No bad blisters.

No obvious wounds. Then she began manipulating his foot. After a period of quiet reflection, the doctor delivered her diagnosis: plantar fasciitis. Her recommended course of action was to buy better silicone boot inserts than the ones he already had and to apply muscle relaxant creme at least a couple of times a day after soaking his foot in warm water. She also recommended doses of high-milligram ibuprofen.

"Can he continue walking the Camino?" I wanted to know. She gave me a stern look. "No long walks for the foreseeable future," she admonished.

I was floored. I myself had previously had plantar fasciitis, but my son's symptoms weren't the same as mine. I would awake and have excruciating pain as soon as my foot touched the floor. The pain would lessen as I limped along, but there was no way I was going to walk several miles every day; it would have been impossible for me. My son didn't wake up with pain. And he did continue to walk. I sort of suspected that "plantar fasciitis" was the diagnosis the doctor would give when nothing else explained foot pain—but I was unjust to the doctor, and also to my son for doubting that he really had plantar fasciitis.

Let me digress briefly to talk about medical treatment in Spain. *Don't worry about going to an emergency room in Spain!* You won't be asked to pay an exorbitant fee that you can't afford. Spain has national health insurance. I tried to pay the hospital at the end of my son's visit, but the staff wouldn't take either cash or a credit card. The checkout staffer told me that I would get a bill in the mail eventually, and that is exactly what happened.

Months (and I mean months) later a bill arrived, from the regional health authority, asking me to pay a very reasonable amount in euros. My only difficulty was in figuring out how to get a money order in euros to the indicated Spanish bank account. My bank and credit union both did international wire transfers, and my credit union offered them in euros. Even with the wire transfer charge added on, the emergency room bill came to less than a hundred dollars. My understanding, perhaps flawed, is that any resident of the EU would have had free treatment.

Also, you will be glad to hear that most towns, even small ones, have a pharmacy (drug store). In Spain, pharmacies are easy to spot since there will be a large green cross mounted to the wall outside. (Clinics and hospitals are identifiable via their red-cross signage, and the pharmacies by their green crosses.) Along the Camino, the pharmacies carry a plentiful supply of blister medication, prominently displayed. And if you have a problem, you can ask the pharmacist for assistance; they are happy to recommend a drug or treatment. I asked the pharmacist for assistance with selecting the best shoe inserts for my son, and she helped us pick out the right ones for him.

Another important item carried by pharmacies is ibuprofen. In Spain, you can get 600 mg tablets over the counter. My son used a lot of them. I used a few. One traveler's account I read said that she popped a 600 mg ibuprofen every morning before setting out, as a prophylactic against the aches and pains the walk was sure to bring.

The bottom line for my son was that the walking part of his Camino was mostly over. I, however, was perfectly fine and wanted to continue. We began a complicated daily tango. Was there a bus to our next stopping place? What about a taxi—how much would that cost? Should I send my son ahead by bus or taxi and walk myself or should I go with him in the bus or taxi? What was the check-out time where we were staying (never an issue previously, because we tried to leave early to avoid the heat)? What was the check-in time at the next place? Where would he hang out if he got to the next town before check-in time? Would he wait for me, or go ahead and eat lunch? And each day we had to sort out many, many other details, all complicated by our inability easily to communicate when apart. (See Chapter 9, "Mistakes," on page 45.)

My son had already walked over 100 kilometers, which is the minimum to receive a Compostela. I wanted to keep on walking, as much as possible, and certainly to walk the last 100 kilometers, which is the most traveled part of the Camino. My son hoped that his foot would be well enough by the time we got to that last 100 kilometers, but it wasn't.

Despite all the aches and pains and my son's plantar fasciitis, I believe we had a successful Camino. Along the way, I heard about other pilgrims who met disaster. They had broken their legs or ankles. Or messed their feet up so badly they couldn't continue. One pilgrim was hit by a tractor. And in Roncesvalles we heard about a woman pilgrim who collapsed on the mountainside and couldn't continue. Eventually a helicopter had to be sent to rescue her, at a cost of over $5,000.

As I write this chapter, I am thinking, "This is going to discourage or turn off a lot of people who are considering the Camino." I hope this account doesn't turn you off, but I also hope it gives you a realistic idea about what walking long distances means, even if you are stopping at a town every night. (Cheryl Strayer's book *Wild* gives a view of what a long walk in remote areas can mean.) It is true that on the Camino you are never *that* far from help—but you might be up a mountain, or on an infrequently traveled part of the Camino, and so not able to access help quickly or easily. I remember that on one shale-strewn section of the trail, when I was going extremely slowly and carefully, planting my feet and my poles with excruciating care at every step, I kept thinking, over and over, "If I fall and hurt myself here, it's going to take them two hours to hike in and get me, and how will they ever manage to get me out? There is no road nearby, no place for an ambulance to reach me." The Camino can be scary.

On the other hand, this remoteness is nothing new, and relatively speaking modern pilgrims have it easy. A pilgrim in the Middle Ages setting out along the Camino was frequently undertaking a two-year trip. Many never returned, having died along the way. The Catholic Church built up a network of "hospitals" along the Camino to care for pilgrims, and medieval organizations like the Knights Templar took as their mission the protection of pilgrims along the route. It was far scarier and more dangerous in centuries past, yet millions of pilgrims set out, with brave hearts and high courage, to make the journey. As a pilgrim on the Camino, you join that long stream of pilgrims.

What should the takeaway be from this chapter? Plan as much as you can. Be ready for aches and pains. Pack basic medicines and blister treatments. Be realistic about what you can expect your body to withstand. Don't be afraid to go to a doctor or clinic if you need to. And keep in mind the expression you will encounter frequently along the Camino: "It's not the destination; it's the journey."

Chapter 9
Mistakes

I MADE A NUMBER OF MISTAKES that cost us financially, emotionally, and physically. I say "emotionally" because the anger and stress occasioned by feeling "taken" or "gypped" caused exactly the opposite kind of feeling I was hoping to experience on the Camino.

The first big mistake was the travel insurance I took out. Quite a while before my trip, I invested in what I thought was top-of-the-line travel insurance that covered me in case of medical emergencies involving either me or close family members. About a month before my trip, but after I had already purchased flights and booked hotels and so forth, a close family member had a medical emergency. I obtained a letter from the relevant doctor saying that he advised me *not* to leave the country as planned but rather to delay my Camino trip. I naively thought that letter would satisfy the insurance company. Instead, the insurance company proceeded to tell me that the medical emergency in question was not a covered occurrence: it was one of the exceptions listed in the exceedingly fine print of the policy. No amount of talking with the insurance company or producing written documentation from medical professionals resulted in a change in the denial.

Once the insurance company denied coverage for the travel delay, I went directly to the airlines and hotels I had booked. They all had ample time to book new passengers and clients for the reserved days and flights—but they still declined to offer refunds or to allow changes in dates. My error was in having booked the least expensive options I could find, which usually carried "no changes" rules. The "no changes" language hadn't worried me, since I had taken out the travel insurance—but after the travel insurance declined to cover my situation, even when all of this was occurring well in advance of the actual travel, I found myself in a pickle.

The cascading effect of the medical emergency and the noncoverage by the travel insurance really cost my wallet. In general, I liked the convenience of using Booking.com when I was making my own hotel arrangements, but I learned the hard way not to go for the no changes option and instead to pay a bit more to keep open the option to cancel until shortly before the check-in date. With life and travel on the Camino as uncertain as they are, keeping your options open is a preferable choice. Of all the hotels I had pre-booked at the "no changes" rate, only one hotel in Madrid, when I produced the letter from the doctor, allowed me to swap the dates for a later time.

An even more aggravating occurrence involved Turkish Airlines. I had booked a flight on Turkish Airlines that used the airport in Santiago de Compostela, which would have been very convenient. Turkish Airlines subsequently decided that that flight would not leave from Santiago but rather from Bilbao, very far away. Turkish Airlines then refused to refund the cost of the flight, despite the fact that the change in the flight had been theirs, not mine.

My overall recommendation is, if you are going to buy travel insurance, be sure to find a policy with "cancel for any reason" coverage. And when you pay in advance for travel and hotels, make sure you are going to be able to cancel or change your dates and get a refund, particularly if you do it well in advance.

My second big mistake involved cell phone usage. I had researched cell phones before departing. After talking to a number of people and my cell phone company, and after taking into account my normal cell phone usage and my son's, I opted for a mixed-use program. I took out the international call plan with my cell company, but decided to purchase a SIM card in Spain for my son. (He uses substantially more data than I do, and would quickly exhaust the limited data allowed by the cell company's international plan.)

Since what I was seeking was for us to be able to keep in touch with each other in Spain when we were not together, for whatever reason, this seemed like a reasonable plan. My mistake was in buying the SIM card at the airport in Madrid when I got off the plane. The company selling the SIM cards totally misrepresented itself. The sales representative said that it would be easy to find one of their stores in all larger towns, in case we needed technical help or to buy additional data. It wasn't true. In fact, we never saw another store for that company the whole two months we were in Spain, and numerous calls to the contact numbers we had been given always went to voice mail. Our calls were never returned.

The company also gave us instructions on how to make calls to and from my son's SIM card-installed cell phone. The instructions did not work. Since we couldn't find any stores and never could telephonically talk to a live human being in order to get technical assistance, we were totally out of luck.

This was an absolute case of "let the buyer beware." If I had to do it over again, I would *not* purchase a SIM card at the airport. It would have been much better to wait and to see which companies were well represented in Spanish cities, then to purchase a SIM card from one of them. There are a number of reputable companies whose names you will hear and see advertised all over Spain. Go for one of those big brands, even if it costs a bit more than a bargain brand, because you will want the access offered by multiple locations across the country.

As it turned out, not being able to phone each other after my son got injured proved to be a daily problem for us. We limped along without good communication capabilities, either between ourselves or with others we met along the Camino. I had been struck, in reading the accounts of other pilgrims, at how often they exchanged numbers and arranged to meet up at the next town for drinks or dinner or just to talk. I had wanted to have that option, but with no national number—which the SIM card was supposed to give us—we didn't have that capacity.

My third big mistake was in trying to mail boxes home through national postal services. I mailed boxes to myself from both France and Spain. Neither box was delivered. I spent many fruitless hours once back home trying to trace the boxes, using the tracking numbers I had been given. No one was ever able to tell me what happened to the boxes, or where they had gone astray. I mourned those boxes for many months.

Here are a few things I learned from that experience. First, if you must send a box home, send it to a friend who can pick it up immediately. Since I was in Spain for almost two months, at least one package seems to have been sent back to Europe when it wasn't claimed promptly at my local post office. Second, you might have better luck if you try sending your package via a courier service like DHL or FedEx than via a national post office. The latter is cheaper, but the former is probably more reliable. And finally, if you possibly can, send your box towards the end of your trip, so you can track its progress back at home and be there to receive it when it arrives.

As I mentioned at the start of this chapter, it wasn't just the financial cost of these choices that hurt. The wasted time—in trying to contact the various companies to make changes, to ask for refunds, to write emails and letters when the requests were denied, to track down my missing boxes—was bad enough, but coupled to the wasted time was the horrible feeling of being taken for a sucker by what had seemed reputable companies or organizations.

I also consider it a mistake to have been slow to take my son for medical assistance after he said his foot was hurting. This point has already been covered in the previous chapter, but to reiterate the main message: do not worry about the cost of medical coverage while you are on the Camino. Doctors and clinics are a lot more reasonably priced than in the United States, and along the Camino the clinical staffs are very used to dealing with the medical problems that pilgrims develop.

Chapter 10
Food and Drink Along the Way

MANY YEARS AGO, I took a trip to Spain along with my mother and cousin. We drove a circular route, starting in Madrid, then heading south to Toledo and Granada; next west through Andalucía to Cordoba and Seville; then north to Merida and Salamanca; and, finally, back to Madrid. Altogether, we were in Spain about a month. It was a wonderful trip, but one thing provoked negative comments after a couple of weeks—Spain was very homogeneous in its food. The same dishes appeared on the menus in Seville as in Toledo or Merida. When asparagus was in season, it seemingly was on menus all over Spain. And there weren't many "foreign" restaurants, or even much regional variety in Spanish dishes.

On my Camino pilgrimage, I again noticed the similarity in menus. There are a wider variety of restaurants available in Spain today than there were 35 years ago, with pizza and Italian restaurants available in most good-sized towns, along with Chinese food. Still, even in large cities you won't find the variety of restaurants you can find in a medium-sized U.S. city, and you won't find the regional or local variation you taste in the USA.

On the other hand, the Spanish menu includes some food that is not commonly found on U.S. menus—such as rabbit and quail. Of course, you can find rabbit and quail at some high-end, gourmet-focused restaurants in the United States, but in Spain these dishes turn up at local restaurants.

Keeping that in mind, here are some notes on food and drink along the Camino.

First, along the Camino you will probably often order the pilgrim's menu. The good points of these menus are that the food is inexpensive and abundant. The bad: you will tire of being offered the same options day after day.

By abundant, I mean a variety of courses, with two or three options for each course. A pilgrim's menu will generally offer a starter (such as soup, salad, or fried squid), a main course (paella or a chicken or beef dish), dessert (egg custard or rice pudding), and a drink (a soft drink or glass of wine)—all for a modest price. Most pilgrims seem to go for these menus, with an occasional splurge at a more expensive place to break up the monotony of the choices.

My son and I usually opted for the pilgrim's menu. Sometimes those menus included my favorite Spanish dishes (below), and sometimes they didn't. When they did, I usually chose them. But some of these favorite dishes we had to seek out. Here are some dishes I recommend you sample while in Spain.

Starters

Gazpacho. The famous cold soup of Spain, with a tomato base and lots of diced vegetables such as cucumbers and onions, which are either already included in the gazpacho or can be added as "sprinkles." On a hot day, after a long walk, I'd give a sigh of happiness whenever gazpacho was an option for lunch. I wish it had always been there, but it wasn't. When you see it on a menu, don't pass it up.

Jamon Serrano (**Serrano ham**). Thinly sliced smoked ham. It is frequently served as an appetizer along with Manchego cheese or melon. This makes a great starter and is very typically Spanish.

Main Courses and Vegetables

Paella. The national dish of Spain, this is a rice-based dish, with its saffron-flavored rice giving the dish its distinctive yellow color. (It has always been a mystery to me how saffron, which looks like brick-red butterfly antennae, will change the color of white rice to yellow rather than red.) Paella is the one Spanish dish that does have variations. Similar in some ways to Louisiana jambalaya, almost anything—meat, seafood, sausage—can be added to a paella, but some varieties always include certain ingredients. *Paella Valenciana* (paella Valencia style) always includes chicken and is probably the most common paella variety you will find. *Paella de Mariscos*—or seafood paella—is also very common. Shrimp, mussels, and squid are usually added to *Paella de Mariscos*. I love paella, and suggest you try all the varieties. Don't be squeamish. You might find, despite what you think, that you like squid when it is cooked in a paella.

Cochinillo Asado (**roast suckling pig**). In *Iberia*, Michener recounts his search for the perfect *cochinillo asado*. Like Michener, you should take on the challenge of finding a perfect roast pork. The best I have ever had was not along the Camino but rather in Toledo—but I kept trying to find one even better, as Michener did.

Alcachofas (**artichokes**). A vegetable that the Spanish love and eat much more frequently than Americans do. *Alcachofas* come on salads and in paellas.

Esparagos (**asparagus**). Spain has a special variety of white asparagus. If you see it on a menu, order it!

Gambas al Ajillo (**shrimp in garlic sauce**). This mouthwatering dish has shrimp swimming in garlic butter. Nothing better, at least to my taste buds.

Calamares Fritos (**fried squid**). Squid is available everywhere, even far inland. The Spanish love squid, and you might come to enjoy it too. Think of it sort of like the onion rings of Spain. The Spanish know how to cook it, and it doesn't taste rubbery the way it often does in the USA.

Pulpo (**octopus**). What I have said about squid goes for octopus too. Octopus is delicious if cooked properly.

Percebes (**barnacles**) **and Other Unusual Seafood.** With its long Atlantic and Mediterranean coastlines, Spain has fish and squid available throughout the country. However, some seafood—like barnacles—are not that frequently found and must be sought out on the menus of seafood restaurants along the coasts. If you are an adventurous eater, try some of the more unusual offerings. Despite the unappetizing English names (like "barnacles") attached to the items, the dishes are usually wonderful —and, I should mention, can be expensive.

DESSERTS

Flan. Egg custard with caramelized sugar. "Custard" sounds yucky to my ears, but "flan" sounds scrumptious. This is a dish whose English translation does it no justice. Flan is my favorite of all Spanish desserts.

Arroz con Leche. Another dessert whose translated name—rice in milk—doesn't do it justice. *Arroz con Leche* is sweet and is topped with a sprinkling of cinnamon. Think of that cinnamon toast your father may have made you when you were a child and you'll get the idea of how something essentially bland (toast or rice) can, with the help of sugar and cinnamon, metamorphose into a delicious treat.

Marzipan and *Turón* (nougat). Having been raised a Catholic, I always have an irreligious taste memory when I eat marzipan: it is like a host melting on my tongue. Turón is sturdier and chock full of nuts. You'll have to seek out these sweets at sweet shops, which thankfully are plentiful in towns and cities. Both marzipan and turón can be expensive.

Manchego (cheese). The most famous Spanish cheese, firm and somewhat salty. Manchego can appear on the menu in a number of places—as a starter paired with fruit or ham or as a dessert course at the end of the meal.

DRINKS

Spain has a wide variety of special drinks that you can enjoy. An interesting fact is that in Spain a soft drink will cost you as much as or more than a beer. As a young woman living in Barcelona, I always thought that paying so much for a coke was crazy and just encouraged people to drink too much alcohol. Nowadays, with doctors and nutritionists warning about the dangers of colas, I have to think that maybe the Spanish got their pricing right after all.

Sangria. My personal favorite is sangria. For me, nothing is better than sitting in a plaza with a pitcher of sangria and a good book or novel about Spain, watching people stroll by while I sip sangria and read. It's heaven, and it can be experienced frequently along the Camino. My favorite new spot is sitting on the plaza outside the cathedral in Santiago, watching all the pilgrims race the last few steps to the burial place of St. James. On my Camino tour, I came across a new sangria variant—or at least, new to me. Made with sparking white wine instead of red, some prefer this as a lighter, more refreshing kind of sangria.

Rioja Wine. Rioja wine is famous, and justifiably so. You can savor it all along the Camino.

Cava. Spanish sparkling wine is called "cava." (In France it is champagne, in Italy prosecco, but in Spain it is cava.) It's fun to have cava for a special occasion, and it is not as expensive as you might expect.

Licor 43. Spain's distinctive liqueur. It tastes of almonds and is truly delicious. A good drink to sip after an excellent supper or when you are sitting around in a bar chatting with friends.

Pacharán. This is a liqueur that I discovered on my Camino trip. It is slightly licorice tasting. I don't like licorice, but I really like *Pacharán.* Give it a try. It is distinctive.

The Spanish in general seem to prefer their own cuisine, hence the homogeneity of the menus throughout Spain—but Spain is not immune to international trends and tastes. You will find hamburgers (*hamburguesas*) and French fries (*papas fritas*) on many menus. Indeed, if you eat the pilgrim's menu, *papas fritas* will usually accompany your main course. Since I am not much of a fan of fried foods, I'd usually ask the waiter to substitute salad for the papas fritas, but once in a while I would succumb and order a heaping pile of

French fries. Maybe I needed the salt after another sweaty walk—or maybe I was just hungry for a bit of home.

My best advice about eating and drinking in Spain is to be a risk-taker. Never tried oxtail soup? It's really good. Never tasted rabbit? Here's your chance. Like Michener, while in Spain I seek out the "perfect" memorable dish or new drink. On my Camino trip, I feasted on *percebes* in Finisterre ("end of the earth") at the conclusion of my journey, and found *sangria de cava* and *Pacharán*, both new to me, entirely to my liking. If only I had a *jarra de sangria* (jug of sangria) with me right now! *Buen apetito!*

Chapter II
On Memory

MEMORY IS A TRICKY THING. I learned this first hand, many years ago, when I was the victim of violent crime and had to testify in court more than a year after the attack. Thanks to this early alert that my memory alters "facts" over time, I have always been interested in memory and how the brain works. One of my frequent traveling companions, an older cousin, has a fabulous memory. Years later, she can accurately recall the names of towns and people and the dates we visited places. I can't. That is one of the reasons I started keeping travel journals, so that I could go back and check the information my brain dredges up, or doesn't, for accuracy.

On the other hand, my own particular brain is very good at synthesis. I can take a lot of facts and integrate them, seeing big patterns. That ability also helps me to pick out anomalies in the pattern. Not too long ago, for example, I made my first visit to China. While there, I noted, in city after city we visited, a strange fad raging among Chinese youth. Mostly females, but also some males, were sticking long hairpins topped by small plastic flowers or insects, especially ladybugs or caterpillars or butterflies, into their hair. These long hairpins would bend and sway as their wearers moved, so that over the heads of crowds in the streets ladybugs and butterflies would dance. I bought several of these hairpins and brought them home, telling my family and young relatives about the fad. Within days of my return, a relative found on the Internet a story in a major news source about this new fad. I had been, thanks to the way my brain works, ahead of the curve with a small travel scoop for my family.

This digression on memory is by way of introduction to these next few chapters on the best and the worst of the Camino. As I write this, a year after my walk in Spain, these are the memories, both good and bad, that have bubbled up to the surface. I believe they are accurate, or as accurate as my memory and my travel journal allow.

Chapter 12
The Almond Man

FOR THOSE WHO WALK THE CAMINO, the Meseta ranks as either the part of the walk they liked most, or the segment they loathed. It is a long, flat section of the trail, a high plain. If you don't like climbing hills or mountains, then the Meseta is a welcome respite from what seems to be the endless daily grind of going up and down slippery slopes. For those who hate it, the Meseta's sameness is boring and seems a waste of limited time.

Our walk across northern Spain coincided with an intense heat wave with temperatures that hadn't been seen in decades. We were lucky in encountering only one downpour in our seven weeks of walking, but we also had the cooling touch of drizzle against our faces on a couple of occasions. The song in the musical *My Fair Lady* about the rain in Spain being on the plain is definitely wrong, or at least it was for the period we were walking on the plain. For the most part, the days were incredibly and unusually hot, a topic that almost every Spaniard we met immediately brought up.

There we were, slogging along the Camino on a very hot June day. The trail was flat (thank goodness!), not too stony (for once!), and compared to much of the Camino was easy walking. But the sun was brutal, bearing down on us as we trudged along. As always, I was wearing a wide-brimmed hat, long sleeves, and long pants. My skin can't take direct sun, and certainly not in the inferno that was Spain in June 2016. Other walkers, many attired in shorts and tank tops, overtook and passed me from time to time. I was carrying a daypack with a hydration (water) insert. In my cargo pants pockets were maps; my passport; a small guidebook; and odds and ends, like a bandana and gum. Weighed down with these possessions, having sweated through my shirt under the daypack, with my sunglasses continually sliding down my nose due to perspiration, I stumbled along, just concentrating on putting one foot in front of the other and trying not to stub my toes on the rocks malevolently camouflaged near the surface of the trail.

As always, my son, James, lagged far behind me. Although forty years younger, healthy and strong, he always managed to walk slower than I did, which was amazing, considering how slowly I walked. (My whole time on the Camino, I think I passed two other pilgrims, one of whom was handicapped.) I knew that James, way behind me, was also suffering in the extreme heat, carrying as he was his own backpack as well as an unwieldy guitar.

The heat shimmered in front of me whenever I looked up. The dust clogged my mouth and nose, so every so often I took a pull on the plastic tube of the hydration pack. Some pilgrims overtook me with handkerchiefs over their mouths and noses. Occasional butterflies fluttered around, but in general the Meseta offered little to tease or delight the eye. The crops growing in the trailside fields were uniformly green, though as clouds moved across the sky the green color varied from emerald to olive green to a light, fresh green color. I stopped several times to try to capture those various green shades in a photograph, but my phone couldn't seem to capture the subtle color variations. Every once in a while, I got a whiff of the suntan lotion that I had applied to my hands and neck.

Up ahead, off in the distance, I saw a car pulled off on the side of the road. It was one of those old-fashioned hump-backed Citroen *Deux Chevaux* (two pistons) that were so prevalent in the 1970s Spain I had visited, but were relatively rare nowadays. As I got closer, I noticed that a man was waiting beside the *Deux Chevaux*, standing out in the full sun. I could see that the two girls who had passed me some way back had stopped by the man. What was going on? Maybe his car has broken down, and he was asking them to carry his plea for assistance to the next small town? Or maybe he was selling something?

Near-sighted as I am, I was unable to see exactly what was happening up ahead with the girls and the man. Him stopping in the middle of nowhere to sell something seemed unlikely. On the other hand, a vendor selling popsicles or ice cones or anything remotely cold would probably be patronized by everyone passing, even the most impecunious. The girls moved off, still far ahead. I was glad to realize that my "Danger, Will Robinson! Danger!" antenna could be retracted. Whatever his presence by the side of the road signified, the man didn't seem to be anyone I needed to worry about.

Finally, I drew close to the man, who I could now see was elderly. He stretched out a hand to me, and I extended my own hand. Instead of shaking my hand, as I had expected, he dropped a handful of shelled almonds into my palm. I looked into his face, brown and lined like a felled branch from the big oak tree in my front yard back home. Most *peregrinos* (pilgrims) can't speak much Spanish, so, clearly, he was used to a wordless handing over of the almonds. A smiling *gracias* was probably the most he usually got in return.

I speak Spanish, so I stopped to chat with him. (I latch on to any and all excuses for a rest stop.) He told me that he came out to this spot most days, and dispensed almonds to those who passed by. Since this was not a heavily traveled section of the Camino, he had long intervals between the departure of one walker and the arrival of the next. While waiting, he stood rooted by the roadside under that burning sky. He said that he never remembered June being this hot, and he offered me water, which I declined. While we chatted, he cracked almonds, getting them ready for the next person to arrive. As it happened, I knew that my son would be the next pilgrim to come along, and I wondered if the aged Spaniard would offer almonds to a man too. Perhaps he just liked interacting with young foreign girls, though he offered me almonds and I was hardly young. Compared to him, however, I still counted as a spring chicken.

By the time my son slouched up, the man, distracted by talking to me, had only cracked about half a handful of almonds. He handed over to James a fistful of almonds still in the shell. I wondered if James's hands were strong enough to crack open the almonds unaided by a tool of some sort. With James's arrival, I bid The Almond Man farewell and started to walk off. The Almond Man reached out to me with an extra gift, a foil-wrapped chocolate. Clearly this was a special gift, kept in reserve by The Almond Man for the *peregrino* or *peregrina* who took the time to chat with him.

A friend later questioned how the chocolate could not have melted in that fierce heat. I can tell you that the chocolate, once turned over to a pilgrim, inevitably made a quick journey to a hungry mouth. As to how the chocolates survived in the car prior to being handed over, I can only attribute it to being a small modern miracle.

Chapter 13
The Truffle Hunter

IN READING OTHER PILGRIMS' TALES of the Camino, I learned that a surprising number of them have had a romantic experience of some sort while walking. This is as close as I got to anything romantic.

My experience with Europe has been that Europe in general beats the USA in terms of public transportation. Before actually walking the Camino, I supposed that there would be a bus to get from one small town to the next. Or perhaps a train. It therefore came as a great surprise to me to find out, after my son's foot injury, that public transportation was in short supply along the French route of the Camino.

Occasionally, between the bigger towns, there would in fact be a bus, and almost always a queue of Camino walkers waiting to catch it. For whatever reason—injury, tiredness, shortness of time—walkers will decide to hitch a ride on public transportation for a while. (When I was young, hitchhiking was common in Spain, and I myself hitch-hiked around southern Spain. At some point, Spain outlawed hitch-hiking, and I didn't see a single hitchhiker on this trip.) For many of the smaller towns, unfortunately, there was no bus at all. I asked all along the way, and was told that there had been buses in the past, but the government had discontinued them. No one could explain why the government had cut bus service, but with the population so low in rural Spain it was easy to speculate that either the service did not cover costs or else the buses were more needed on other, more populous routes.

If one needs to travel from one small town to another by a method other than walking, as we did, the only option is to take a taxi. Even the smallest towns had a taxi, or else there would be a taxi in the next town that could come and pick us up. The hostels and bars along the Camino always knew how to contact a taxi, and luckily the taxi fares were standardized and well-regulated, with the cost determined by mileage.

One day we stopped for a late lunch in a small town. My son, cradling his foot in his hands, said that he didn't think he could walk anymore because his foot was hurting too much. The café where we were eating was part of a complex that included a bar and some inexpensive rooms mainly booked by Camino walkers. We were seated at an outside table, so after lunch I went into the bar to ask the barman about buses. He told me that there was no bus to the next town, Castrojeriz, so I asked him about the availability and price of a taxi. At that point, a man sitting at the bar interrupted, offering to drive me to the next town.

On most occasions I would have rejected this offer out of hand. Getting into a car with a strange man is not something I do. In this case, however, I had my 25-year-old son waiting outside for me. I chatted with the man, who said he was going in that direction and wouldn't mind giving me a lift, so long as I could wait for him to finish his beer. I accepted his offer.

Once he finished his beer, we went outside. When he saw my son rise and join me, the man's face fell about a mile. He had obviously thought I was alone, and the addition of my son to the party was not to his liking. His reaction made me doubt his intentions, but my son was relieved not to have to walk any more that day and seemed almost joyful about getting a free ride to the next town, so we got in the car. The man introduced himself as Angel. A dog was waiting for him in the car.

Angel was average—not tall, not short. Not fat or thin. Middle aged. He had the typical Spanish full head of dark hair. His one distinctive characteristic was bad teeth. Some were missing, others black with rot.

As we drove along, chatting in Spanish, I tried to keep him talking by asking questions. The best way, in my experience, to deflect unwanted questions about oneself is to ask questions of the other person. (At times, the Spanish will ask you embarrassingly personal questions, seemingly abiding by a different social code as to what constitutes polite and impolite conversation. "How much is your salary?" they will ask, or "Why doesn't your son look like you?" They think nothing of admiring some possession of yours and then asking, "How much did it cost?") I did not want to give Angel any personal details about myself.

More than once during the drive, Angel bemoaned his lack of a wife.

"That dog in the back seat, that is Cherie. She is my wife," he told us.

Within a relatively short period of time, Angel said that he would like to take us to his house. *Whoa! Danger, Will Robinson! Danger!* He said that he lived in a house with a ruined church next door, which he owned. He needed to stop by the house briefly to check on his dog. Not the dog in the back seat, but a different dog. Moreover, he would be delighted to show us his house and the church.

As best I could, I tried politely to decline—but the man insisted, saying that he needed to see about his dog. Then he began to tell us that he hunted truffles and had a large cache of them at his house. He wanted to show us the truffles.

My son, riding in the back seat, perked up at the mention of truffles. At an earlier age he had considered studying culinary arts and becoming a chef. During that period of time he watched a lot of cooking shows like *Top Chef*. He began to ask The Truffle Hunter everything about truffles—where he found them, what types he found, how much he sold them for, who bought them. The truffle questions emerged endlessly from my son, an amazing development considering his normal reticence with strangers. I relaxed and let the conversation flow back and forth between the front and back seats.

I only had one truffle-related question. "Do you use a pig to find the truffles? I've heard that they are supposed to have excellent noses for truffles and can root them up easily."

"That's true, but I don't use a pig. My dog is an excellent truffle hunter. A dog like him is a very valuable commodity, and that is why I have to take good care of my dog and stop to make sure he is OK in this heat."

How could I argue with that? The man's livelihood was at stake, and in addition my son was enthusiastic about seeing The Truffle Hunter's truffle stash.

We stopped at The Truffle Hunter's house. It was a typical Spanish rural dwelling, modest in size and just one story. Probably at least a couple of hundred years old, its grey weathered stone was not painted. And right next to it was, as he had said, a beautiful ruined, roofless church, which in the days of the Romantic period would have been considered mysterious and alluring, a big temptation to young ladies like those in Jane Austen's *Northanger Abbey*. OK, I admit it, owning your own ruined medieval church was an attractive proposition, at least for a history major like me.

The Truffle Hunter began to extol his house's excellent qualities.

"It is old, but very comfortable. As you can feel, it is quite cool even in the hottest summer. Let me show you around."

My son eagerly followed him all over the house, including the bedrooms, but I planted myself in the public rooms and stayed there.

After The Truffle Hunter offered a full house tour with continuing commentary about his single and lonely existence, broken only by the company of his dogs (he didn't mention beers down at the café), I had a pretty good idea of what was going on. My son was blissfully unaware.

"Can we see the truffles?" asked my son.

The Truffle Hunter went into the kitchen and returned with a rather large plastic container. He popped off the lid, and there nestled inside was a large mound of brown and tan mushrooms. A rich, loamy aroma escaped from the plastic tub. "This one container," he said, "holds about 2,000 euros worth of truffles. And I have several of them."

A very trusting guy, I thought, *to leave such valuable property in his refrigerator for any thief to loot from this isolated, rural home with no alarm except for a dog out there somewhere.*

The Truffle Hunter explained that truffles have a short shelf life. When he had a large enough stock, he would drive to the closest big town and sell his truffles to chefs.

"I go from restaurant to restaurant. The chefs know me, and they buy directly from me." So that was how he supported himself. (Too bad he didn't spend any of his income on his teeth.)

He tried to detain us longer.

"Would you like me to show you around the property?"

"Thank you, but no." I sort of wanted to see the truffle-hunting dog, but I wanted most of all to get out of there.

"Do you want some wine or a beer?"

My son was on the brink of saying "yes" when I interrupted. "Thank you so much, but I think we need to leave. If we don't get to our booked room fairly quickly, they might give it away to someone else."

The Truffle Hunter frowned, but then turned and went outside to check on his up-until-now ignored dog. He puttered around the house doing a few other tasks, then announced that he was ready to drive us to our hotel.

Energized by seeing all those truffles, my son continued to pepper The Truffle Hunter with questions while we drove to the hotel. That made me happy, because it took some of the conversational pressure off of me.

We arrived at our destination. Having given up his original goal by this time, The Truffle Hunter set a new one. "I know that I said there would be no charge for the ride, but that was just for the ears of the barman. It is illegal for private citizens to charge people for rides, but the cost is actually 20 euros. That is about half of what a taxi would have cost you."

I happily passed over the 20 euros, and both of us bade goodbye to The Truffle Hunter.

Over dinner, my son asked me why I had seemed so eager to get away from The Truffle Hunter's house.

"Didn't you see his face fall when he saw you were with me? He thought I was alone. Didn't you hear how he kept saying in the car that he wasn't married but really would like to be? Didn't you hear him tell us all the wonderful aspects of his house? And didn't you hear him tell us about his wonderful truffle income?"

"Yeah, I heard all that. So what?"

"He was clearly hunting for the ultimate truffle: a rich American wife."

I still think of The Truffle Hunter every time I see truffles mentioned on a menu. I briefly ponder what might have been, had I been in the mood for romance. I still do regret rushing away and never stepping foot inside the romantic, ruined church.

Chapter 14
She Who Laughs Last

MY TRAVELING COMPANION for the Camino trip was my son, James.

James is now 27 years old, but during his childhood he was preternaturally interested in his appearance. I grew up with four brothers and a male cousin, and, as children, none of the five of them ever cared in the least about how they looked. They always had crew cuts until they got to be teenagers. My mother bought herself a set of hair clippers and served as the barber.

As for clothes, parochial school uniform requirements took care of clothing for most days, while blue jeans and t-shirts served for after-school hours and weekends. My brothers only needed a nice pair of pants, a white shirt, and a tie for mass on Sundays.

That was my experience growing up with five boys, and that is what I expected would be the case with James. Was I ever wrong!

From the time he was five or six, James cared about his hair. I mean, really cared. It began during the era when the Bruce Willis spiky hair style was in vogue. James had to have that haircut. He also had to have exactly the right hair gel, and, of course, the most expensive brand. And he spent eons in front of his bathroom mirror making sure his hair looked just right.

At first, I tried to josh or shame him out of this fixation by noting that he spent a lot more time primping than I did. I hate that word "primping." I hated it when my mother used to say, "Julie, stop primping and get out here right now." I naively thought that bringing out the big gun "primping" word—even more damning when applied to a boy than a girl—would have the same effect on James as it used to have on me, but it didn't faze him in the slightest.

The spiky look was just the first of many styles. He colored his hair several different colors over the years, had it rock-star long for a long time, went through a phase of not combing it for days, and tried out any new style that came down the pike, including mullets and other bizarre styles. No amount of telling him that he was blessed with thick, curly hair that most men would die for and that his hair looked superb at a medium length that showed his curls, which girls would love, seemed to make an impression. Eventually, I gave up commenting about or objecting to whatever he wanted to do with his hair. Except going blond. I told him he would have to wait until he was 21 to ruin his hair by coloring it blond.

My next shock came about clothes. It didn't really erupt until sixth grade, but, when it did, the issue was volcanic. We had moved back to the Washington, DC, area from overseas, and James was in his first year of middle school at a public school. No uniforms. Before the first week was out, James was telling me he needed different clothes. His pants were wrong. His shirts were wrong. Even his shoes were wrong. I resisted. He had perfectly good school clothes in his closet. He continued demanding new clothes. At a certain point, after James had taken the emotion to a wholly unexpected level, I gave in. Thinking about it, I realized that the constant moving from city to city that my job required was hard for him. He was always the new kid, always wearing styles that were "out," always having to figure out how to fit in.

I took him shopping, and I let him pick out his school clothes and an exorbitantly expensive (at least to my mind) pair of sneakers. James never did manage to fit in at that school, and before long he was saying that he wanted to go back overseas again right away. Which we did, as soon as the school year ended.

Once overseas, his new best friend was sporting the baggy pants style. You know the one I mean, when boys wear trousers two sizes too big, then let the pants hang down so far that their underpants show. Once again, James had to have new, in this case too large, clothes. "I'll grow into them," he would cajole. Luckily, he was in a private school that required uniforms and didn't permit the baggy pants look, so I didn't have to fight with him on school days. Weekends were another story. "Pull up your pants, James," became my refrain. "Your crotch is down to your knees. How can you walk?" I sometimes asked him. I knew better than to say, "Why do you want to wear a style made popular by gangsters and convicts?"

After years of this tussling over his clothes, James finally just started looking at me and saying, "Get used to it."

Fast forward to the Camino. I had months to plan for the trip, and consulted lots of people and read books on what to pack. James was a last-minute addition to the trip, so we had to hustle around to stores just before we left in order to get him what he needed: good hiking boots, merino socks, walking sticks, a hat against the sun, a backpack, a daypack, etc. For each purchase, I told him what was recommended, but James, as usual, preferred his own sense of style to what others thought.

I tried particularly hard to get him to pick out cargo pants. My Camino mentor had strongly recommended such pants, telling me that the large front pockets were the perfect place to carry a map or guidebook and travel documents. Cargo pants made it easy to access items quickly. No need to take off a daypack, rummage through it, find the item, then put the daypack back on. That sounded like good advice to me, and for myself I bought two pairs of cargo pants. I found them in the men's section of a sporting goods store. They were lightweight, quick to dry, and equipped with the all-important large front pockets. In short, they seemed perfect for the Camino. I tried to steer James in the same direction, but he resisted. No cargo pants for him.

Once in Spain and walking, I loved my cargo pants. Just as my mentor had said, I could carry my route book in one pocket, and my passport in the other. Very convenient. Only a small problem emerged. It turned out that, with the weight of a book and other items in the pockets, the pants sagged.

My first day of wearing the pants on the trail, James told me, "Mom, pull your pants up." I did. Of course, they sagged again. James generally walked behind me on the Camino, so he had a good view of the tops of my cotton underwear.

"Mom, I can see your underwear." I pulled them up again.

Five minutes later, "Mom, you need to buy a belt." This went on for several days, every time I wore the cargo pants.

Finally, with a bubble of happiness rising in my chest, I turned around to him and said, "Get used to it."

Postscript: I did eventually buy a belt, because constantly tugging my pants up was a hassle. Still, I had that one, shining moment of payback. This is not the sort of emotion the Camino is supposed to evoke, but it sure felt good.

Chapter 15
The Baby Carriage

ALONG THE CAMINO, you see every sort of travel group. Singles, pairs, couples holding hands, groups, large groups, even one very pregnant young woman. Parents with children. People walking with dogs.

I always looked over the children closely. I myself found the walking very strenuous. How would a six-year-old kid manage it? One time we met and chatted with a threesome on bikes: father, mother, and son, who was about ten years old. I knew how James had hated biking uphill, so I was curious about how this boy was doing on the many hills and mountains of the Camino. His parents both averred that he was doing great. They had just started the Camino, so he had only had one day of biking so far, but he had done wonderfully that first day. The boy himself seemed happy. He was proud of staying up with his parents, and even boasted of being in the lead at times. Clearly this was an adventure he was relishing. The other children we saw also seemed happy as they walked, skipped, and ran along. I overheard no whining or complaining.

I became used to seeing all sorts. Even so, I was taken aback one day at what I saw. James and I were struggling down a steep, scree-covered slope. You had to really keep focused, because the slippery rocks under your feet made every step treacherous. Walking sticks were a huge help, and I don't know how many times I would have fallen without them.

This, for me, was dangerous going. I had already broken my ankle once years previously, and the last thing I wanted was another broken ankle or leg. If I fell and injured myself along this largely inaccessible trail, how would emergency workers even get to me, much less carry me out? I went extremely slowly, planting my walking sticks securely, carefully putting each foot down and testing the footing before fully shifting my weight onto that foot, and always being ready for the slides that inevitably happened despite my care. This was tiring and anxiety-producing hiking, so I stopped often to look around. I needed to remind myself of the beauty of the countryside. And to remember the reasons why I was doing the walk.

Thanks to my frequent stops, I had plenty of time to observe these two guys toiling up the slope towards us. Seeing them was unusual for two reasons. First, they were going in the wrong direction. That is, they were headed away from, not towards, Santiago de Compostela. The great majority of pilgrims walk to Santiago. Only a tiny fraction walks home again, or back to their starting point. In our two months of walking, we only saw a handful of pilgrims headed back.

The second reason the two men were worth observing was that they were pushing a baby carriage. Uphill! On this scree-filled slope! It was hard enough going downhill. Going up, pushing that carriage, must have been hell. I kept wondering about what sort of crazy guys would be bringing a baby on this trip. The only explanation I could think of was that maybe they were locals, not pilgrims, and had no choice about routes to get home.

We approached closer and closer. Finally, we stopped, just uphill from them. The hood of the baby carriage was up, shielding the baby from the strong Spanish sun.

Usually pilgrims pass each other by with a cheery *"Buen Camino!"* exchanged. Occasionally a pilgrim will ask a question about the route ahead—how far to the next town, or whether the other pilgrim had seen a certain individual on the Camino?

After I exchanged a few words with this particular pair, it was clear that these two men were foreign pilgrims, not locals. I continued to wonder about what in the world they were doing bringing a baby on this trip. While I wondered, I minded my manners and did not ask them any of the questions that were fizzing in my head. *Where's the mom? How were they feeding the baby? Where were they staying?* The pilgrim hostels wouldn't take babies, I was pretty sure.

Finally, after a few minutes of chatting about the weather and the route, I broached what I really wanted to know.

"Are you on your way home?"

"Yes," one of the men replied, "we are going back to our starting point in France."

"*My God,*" I thought, "*over the Pyrenees with a baby carriage?*"

"Can I see the baby?"

"Sure. Take a look."

I made my careful way down the slope, stopping by the carriage. I peeked in, to see a mass of puppies curled up together. Only then did I notice a bitch sheltering in the shade under the baby carriage.

"Goodness! What's this?"

"Seven puppies. Born on the Camino."

"How old are they?"

"A week."

I looked down at the mama dog under the carriage with pity. She'd had to walk to Santiago pregnant, whelp seven pups, then turn around and go back the other direction while nursing her pups. I wondered, but didn't ask, where they had acquired the baby carriage. And what about dog food for the new mom? I didn't see any in evidence.

I looked at the mama dog again, and wished I had the courage to tell the two guys that they should be giving her a ride in the carriage too. Instead, I just said a heartfelt "*Buen Camino y buena suerte!*" and moved on down the slope. I am still wondering if this party of ten all made it home OK. And I still wish that I had taken a photo of the pups in the baby carriage, the littlest pilgrims I saw.

Chapter 16
The Best of the Camino: Roncesvalles, Burgos, León

SPAIN WAS MY SECOND-EVER FOREIGN COUNTRY to visit, and by the age of twenty-three I thought I knew it quite well. When I dropped out of college at twenty, I went to Portugal to see a friend—and ended up staying there for a year and a half, at first working in a small hotel and later Teaching English as a Foreign Language (TEFL) for a year. I was living off the economy, which basically means I had little money and for that reason I had to live like the Portuguese lived, with few amenities and fewer luxuries. My one indulgence was to travel whenever I could, either within Portugal or to next-door Spain.

One Easter break, I met my then-boyfriend in Madrid. That's a story in itself, with missed meetups at the American Express office, which was the favorite rendezvous spot of young travelers in those days. Besides hitting the highlights in Madrid and falling in love with Velazquez's *Las Meninas* and Bosch's *The Garden of Earthly Delights*, we took a day trip down to Toledo to see the town and the masterpieces there that were painted by another famous artist of the Spanish Renaissance, El Greco. During another school break, my girlfriend and I hitchhiked around southern Spain—Granada, Cordoba, Seville.

After teaching English in Lisbon for a year, I transferred to Barcelona and taught English there, continuing to travel at every opportunity. In Valencia, my boyfriend and I saw the incredible *fallas* (gigantic effigies burned in every plaza in town) during the Feast for San Jose (St. Joseph). We drove to Pamplona for San Fermin, donned the traditional white clothes and red scarves, drank too much cheap red wine out of a leather wineskin, and slept in my car. My boyfriend ran the bulls, of course, and managed to escape safely despite the crush of bodies in the narrow streets. On weekends, I ranged up and down the coast around Barcelona, and at Easter time I went back to Seville for the incredible *Semana Santa* (Holy Week).

About twenty years later I returned to Spain with my mother and my cousin for a grand circle trip, starting in Madrid, then traveling south to Granada, Cordoba, and Seville, then northwards to Merida and Salamanca. Merida had a stunning new museum focused on Roman antiquities and an incredibly well-preserved Roman amphitheater, while Salamanca with its famous-since-the-Middle-Ages university and massive wooden doors was a feast for the eyes, just in walking through its streets.

All in all, I thought I knew Spain well, but I always had that nagging feeling that I needed to do the Camino. If Michener recommended it, it had to be good. With a mindset that I had already seen the best that Spain had to offer, I viewed the Camino as an adventure and a chance to savor Spanish culture, but I wasn't expecting to find out that my knowledge of Spain had big holes in it.

Roncesvalles. I had heard about Roncesvalles—or actually *Roncevaux*, as the French call it—long before. I knew about *The Song of Roland*, probably from first semester French in college. But in my mind, the action in that poem happened in the mountains in France. After all, it was a medieval tale about French knights, in which Roland, the favorite knight of Charlemagne, is betrayed and killed in battle. It's true that Roncesvalles is in the Pyrenees, but it is on the Spanish side of the border, not the French.

Coming down off the mountains into the small town of Roncesvalles feels like descending through the mists of time to an ancient place. Like Brigadoon or other magical places, it seems to appear from nowhere, wrapped in mist and mystery. For those like me who love history, it is a not-to-be-missed town, the setting for one of the great chivalric tales.

Travelers on the Camino still get lost making their way over the Pyrenees, or get caught by sundown while still trekking down the mountain. Roncesvalles Monastery for centuries has tolled its bells to lead pilgrims to safety.

Exploring the Roncesvalles Monastery, its church and chapels, and the town was a treat. I became fascinated with a different hero than Roland, the Navaresse king Sancho VII, who is buried in the Chapel of St. Augustine. Sancho was more than seven feet tall, hence his moniker, "the Strong." He fought in the Battle of Las Navas de Tolosa in 1212, leading his men to an important victory and paving the way for the eventual *Reconquista* (reconquest) of Spain from the Muslims, which wasn't finished until 1492 by Ferdinand of Aragon and Isabella of Castile. Sancho was the brother-in-law of Richard the Lion Hearted, and also fought on Richard's behalf. While Roncesvalles is famous for Roland, it really ought to be famous for Sancho VII, who fought and won against the Muslims—but, somehow, he has not come down through history as "romantic" or memorable, in the way that Roland has, despite *The Song of Roland* being erroneous in one of its principal elements.

Learning more about the true events at the Battle of Roncesvalles in 772 gave me pause for thought. *The Song of Roland* says that the attackers—the treacherous villains who cowardly ambushed and slew the chivalrous Roland and the other French knights—were Saracens (Muslims). That, it seems, is a total slander of Muslims. The actual attackers were Basques, who were enraged by the French sacking of the Basque capital, Pamplona, and the French pillaging of the countryside. Naming Muslims as the enemy rather than the indigenous population (the Basques) may have been politically expedient as part of the overall effort to reconquer Spain and drive the Muslims out of Europe, but it gives me an uneasy feeling about scapegoating. Instead of the 400,000 Saracens who supposedly brought down Roland and the other knights, it was a group of provincials who knew the mountains, were skilled in guerrilla warfare, and were furious about foreigners thinking that they could walk in and take over.

Just thinking about visiting Roncesvalles gives me a shivery feeling. Not the raised-hair scare of a horror movie, but a glimpse of a shadowy past and the tingling of déjà vu. There is a wonderful scene in the movie *Patton* when George C. Scott, as Patton, stands surveying a barren plain, the site of a famous ancient battle. He hears trumpet calls floating on the wind, and catches the sounds of swords clashing on shields. That is the experience I had in Roncesvalles, a glimpse through the veil of time of all those pilgrims coming down the mountain, guided through the mists and the darkness by the lights of the monastery and the mournful sound of its bell.

Roncesvalles is a not-to-be-hurried-through stop on the Camino.

Burgos. In planning our walk on the Camino, I scheduled a rest stop at all the major towns along the way. Besides needing an opportunity to replace whatever had worn out or been left behind and to wash clothes, I wanted a chance to spend a day in these northern Spanish cities. I had already visited Pamplona and was happy to return to Hemingway's favorite bar for a drink and to lounge in the plaza with a *jara* (pitcher) of sangria and a book. Though Pamplona was familiar ground to me, Burgos was new. To be honest, I did not have high expectations. Burgos had the reputation of being a gritty industrial town, and the walk through the outer suburbs to the central city just reinforced that idea. The Burgos Cathedral was therefore an incredible surprise, and while there, I just kept thinking, why doesn't Spain trumpet this cathedral more widely?

One of the conundrums in regards to Spain has to do with its economic trajectory. How could a nation that was once a superpower militarily and an economic dynamo with the wealth of the Americas pouring into its coffers wind up as one of the poorest nations in

Europe? Long ago I heard a lecture about this, the gist of which was that Spain squandered its wealth rather than investing it in the country's infrastructure, businesses, and so forth. Burgos Cathedral gives a concrete illustration of that mistake.

The Cathedral is not particularly impressive on the outside, but the inside is a feast for the eyes. Large, incredibly beautiful wrought-iron screens surround the choir, located in the center of the church, and form a fourth see-through wall on many of the twenty or so chapels that ring the main space. Each one of those wrought iron screens, if in another church or cathedral, would be considered a masterpiece, but in Burgos Cathedral they are everywhere.

Looking at the chapels one by one, I realized that the Cathedral could be the site of an art history course, with each era represented by one or more of the chapels. There was low Gothic, high Gothic, Plateresque, Baroque, Rococo—all of the various artistic styles that came to prominence through the centuries following the Romanesque era. The chapels were largely built by individual noble families, and families hired the best available stone masons, sculptors, and artists to adorn their family chapel. For a family to be able to afford to fund such a chapel was a huge source of prestige; their family name would forever be associated with the chapel, which was built for the greater glory of God and whichever saint was being honored, but also for the greater glory of their own family. Since these chapels were constructed over a long period of time, from 1221 onwards, each chapel reflected the prevailing artistic style of the day. In some chapels, the golden gilding on everything is blinding. In others, there are several masterpieces hanging near each other.

The patrons of each chapel were usually interred in the chapel, so a progression of magnificent tomb art also dazzles the viewer. The most famous figure interred in the cathedral is El Cid, the Castilian knight whose exploits are the subject of Spain's most significant medieval epic poem, *El Cantar de Mio Cid* (The Song of Cid).

The question of what happened to Spain's wealth is obvious in Burgos Cathedral. It went into the glorification of God, by means of pouring fountains of money into this one cathedral, and into other cathedrals and churches throughout Spain. Of course, the chapels also served as status symbols for the noble families, a way to show off their wealth and win immortality. Whether the use of the money for this purpose constitutes "squandering" the money can be debated, in the same way that we can wonder about the Popes pouring money into art instead of feeding the poor—but those who can now view Burgos Cathedral are without a doubt richer for this immense architectural and artistic treasure.

When we staggered out of the cathedral, my son said, "It's overwhelming." Amen to that. I just wished that I had a week to spare so as to spend more time in the cathedral, and an art history specialist with me to help me appreciate what I was seeing. I made do with reading my guidebook and listening in on the talks of the professional guides as I moved slowly around the gigantic cathedral.

León. Whereas Burgos Cathedral is massive, solid, grounded, and golden, the cathedral in León is the opposite—light, airy, cobalt blue and vibrant red. By the time the citizens of León got around to starting their cathedral, Gothic was in full swing, flying buttresses and all. And León embraced that style with verve. Three incredible levels of stained-glass panels line the walls, with very little in the way of supporting stone between the huge panels. The top-most level has rondels, the middle tier scenes from the New Testament, and the bottom row episodes from the Old Testament. It is just jaw-droppingly gorgeous. For anyone like me, raised in Catholic churches with stained glass, this cathedral put everything I had previously seen in the shade. How has the cathedral managed to stay standing all these centuries with such a thin fabric of walls? How did the stained glass survive the Spanish Civil War? Why is this cathedral not better known? All these questions raced through my head.

The guides in León make much of the fact that León and Chartres Cathedrals are neck and neck in regards to the total amount of stained glass incorporated into the structure, and that León surpasses Chartres in the amount of stained glass per square foot. I had not yet seen Chartres Cathedral when I saw León, but I couldn't see how any more stained glass could possibility be squeezed into the walls. Standing in León Cathedral and seeing those amazing biblical scenes in dazzling "technicolor" brought joy to my senses, as I am sure it has done to worshippers throughout the centuries.

I visited León Cathedral on a sunny summer day, with the light pouring through the windows. Michener describes standing outside the church at night, when it was all lit up on the inside, and seeing the glowing windows march towards the sky. I hope to see that view of the windows someday.

The year after I saw León Cathedral, I finally saw Chartres. Both are magnificent, but, in my opinion, León is every bit as outstanding as Chartres and deserves more of an international reputation.

Roncesvalles, Burgos, and León are the three places along the Camino that impressed me the most, but there are many other equally wonderful places to visit. Savor them, don't run past.

Chapter 17
The Worst of the Camino: Shale Hell and Boulder Purgatory

R ONCESVALLES, BURGOS, AND LEÓN are not to be missed, but there are other spots along the Camino that you *should*, if you possibly can, avoid.

In general, the Camino is well marked. Yellow arrows, the symbol of the Camino, appear frequently, pointing the way to Santiago. Occasionally, at an intersection or a Y in the trail, a pilgrim will look around in vain for an arrow. Sometimes, if you look long enough, you will eventually spot a yellow arrow, posted high up on a tree, low down on a fence, or somewhere else not immediately noticeable. At other times, that yellow arrow just isn't there. Whenever you are unsure about the route, it is helpful to have a map in your pocket or backpack so that you can puzzle out whether to go left or right or straight ahead.

Sometimes, after walking a rather long way without seeing a yellow arrow, I would feel anxiety set in. Did I take a wrong turn? Did I miss a yellow arrow directing me to turn left or right? Am I off the Camino? That's why frequent yellow arrows, even along straight stretches, are welcome.

Sometimes you won't see a yellow arrow, but rather a mileage marker, indicating how many kilometers to Santiago from that point. Sightings of those marker stones are also welcome since they both assure a weary pilgrim that she is on the right path and help interested walkers gauge in a rough fashion how many kilometers per hour they are walking.

What the Camino does not have along the Way are indications of danger or degree of difficulty. I believe the Camino should have markings letting pilgrims know about the trail ahead, like ski slopes do. Is this a bunny slope, or a black diamond? Some areas, like along the Meseta, are mostly flat, and would have zero degree of difficulty. Other areas have extreme elevation changes and would rate a much higher degree of difficulty. Of course, such ratings would not tell travelers everything, but common sense can kick in. For example, some pilgrims hate the Meseta because they cross it in high summer, with the sun broiling down and little in the way of shade. Others find it terribly boring for its lack of interesting natural or manmade features. "Degree of difficulty" can be interpreted in different ways, but slip and fall potential is what needs to be posted, in my opinion.

As for me, I am a true flatlander and hate hills and mountains. Yes, I agree that they are beautiful to look at, but I have no desire to climb up or down a hill if I can avoid it. The Camino is no place for someone like me because every day, even while traversing the Meseta, a pilgrim has to conquer the hills and mountains. I would climb and climb, think I was almost at the summit, then stride around a corner and see that I had much more still to climb. Or, I would finally top a hill only to see an even bigger hill looming in front of me. This constant up and down can get very discouraging. You climb up a tall hill, then at the summit see that you have to descent that same hill, then climb another hill to that same height just a little way further along.

At the Visitor Center in Saint-Jean-Pied-de-Port at the start of our journey, I picked up an elevation map. The map divided the Camino into different *stages* (the French word *stage* is usually used for these divisions). The map also showed the elevation changes along the route. I used that elevation map every day. In the morning I would study it, locating our stopping place and figuring out, as best I could, how much climbing I would have to do that day. A good day for me showed few if any elevation changes, a bad day a significant change. Even so, the elevation map could be deceiving. Your daily *stage* might start and end at roughly the same elevation, but along the way you would have climbed and descended four or five quite high hills.

As everyone knows who has walked in hilly country, coming down the hill can be as difficult or even more difficult than going up. It was while on the frequent descents that I came to love my walking sticks. Humans, in becoming bipedal animals, gained the advantage of being able to see over tall grasses and such—but we lost the stability of four legs. I quickly found out how walking sticks gave me back a measure of that stability.

In 1990 in Bogotá, which is itself a very hilly city, I fell and snapped my ankle. I had to have surgery, and the surgeon inserted a metal rod and five screws into my leg. I was younger and slimmer and fitter back then, but even so dragging myself around on crutches for several weeks was a trial I never want to repeat. The fear of falling and breaking a leg or ankle became my nightmare scenario during the trip. I wanted to avoid that outcome at all costs. Going downhill, even more than puffing uphill, I was extremely cautious. Move one pole forward. Step. Move the other pole forward. Make sure both poles are securely anchored and my forward foot on firm ground before moving the other foot forward. Four slow "steps" for every two on flat ground. Even using this slow, precautious method, the ground was often so full of small rocks or shale that I would slip and slide. My poles saved me from numerous falls. The Camino brings in a great deal of revenue for Spain, and the presence of pilgrims has revitalized northern Spain. Small towns have received a needed burst of activity, with pilgrim presence resulting in the opening of new auberges and restaurants and convenience stores. The government of Spain, however, does not seem to invest much in making the Camino better for pilgrims. Most of the work along the Camino seems to be done by the many Camino volunteer support groups, like APOC, which fund upgrades to hostels and trails and so forth. The whole time James and I were walking, we only saw one place where a government "trail improvement" project was underway.

In medieval times, the Catholic Church provided monasteries and "hospitals" all along the way, and organizations like the Knights Templar had the security of pilgrims as their mission. Nowadays, voluntary organizations try to provide services, but much more is needed. For example, the Meseta would be much more hospitable if benches and shade trees were sprinkled along the Camino every few kilometers so that pilgrims could rest for a few minutes in a shady spot. While there are some rest stops along the way, they are generally poorly maintained—with overflowing trash cans, discarded scraps of paper fluttering around, and so forth.

Such improvements to the Camino would make it a much more pleasant walk, but what absolutely positively needs to be done is to repair the really bad spots, or at least to warn travelers that they are facing truly dangerous conditions.

When I think about our journey, I remember two hazardous descents along the way. The first was a steep downhill ravine formed by huge boulders. That way down might be fine for mountain goats, but not for people. The rockiness of the place makes walking sticks virtually useless. There were few spots large enough for a foot as big as mine, so I had to twist and turn and try to find something to grab onto while I gingerly took huge steps down from one boulder to the next, or from one patch of dirt to the next relatively flat space. Sometimes my knees were trembling from fatigue, and I stood frozen trying to figure out what to do. Should I go back up and try to find another way around? (There is always the highway to walk along, which brings its own set of dangers.) How far to the bottom? What should I do?

On very difficult walking days, my son James became a tremendous asset. For most of our walk, James would lag far behind me. I am a slow walker, but even so he would be far behind. Sometimes he would stroll along strumming his guitar, and I could hear the music faintly drifting behind me. Sometimes when I could no longer hear or see him, I would just stop and wait for him to catch up. This gave me a useful rest period and alleviated my concern that he had taken a wrong turn somewhere and was off the trail.

In another chapter, I will be talking about the concept of a "true" pilgrim and what that means. True pilgrims back in the Middle Ages walked both to and from the holy sites, but nowadays most pilgrims only walk towards Santiago and then return home by train or plane or other modern mode. The result of this is that there are few pilgrims returning along the route. Very occasionally one will meet walkers coming in the other direction, and, in such instances, it is practically required to ask "How far to the next town?" before passing each other going in opposite directions, with both persons offering a *Buen Camino* to the other.

Since there were essentially no returning pilgrims from whom to glean such information, sometimes the only way to gather route information was, like in pioneer days, to send a scout ahead. With groups traveling together, I frequently noticed the fast walkers phoning back information to the slower members of their party. James walked even slower than I did, so he could not serve as my scout. And even had he walked ahead of me, my purchase of the wrong SIM card and call plan meant that he couldn't phone me with updates.

On difficult days like the one with the boulder ravine, James would catch up with me. He would then take the lead and have to descend through this boulder valley assessing what lay ahead, then climb back up to meet me and report conditions. He would accompany me back down the pathless slope, pointing out good landing sites for my big feet and safe ways to traverse a boulder.

I came away from this descent thinking that there should be a sign at the top of it that said something like, "Descend at your own peril. This is a very dangerous path. It is recommended that travelers take the longer route along the highway instead." And the sign should be boldly marked with some sort of symbol that travelers would recognize. A skull-and-crossbones would work, though boulders rather than pirates are what could cause one to fall and break one's neck. Ski slopes use a black diamond for their most difficult and dangerous slopes, and the Camino should have a similar symbol—maybe a red stick figure falling down.

The boulder descent day was a bad day, but it wasn't the worst. The worst was the seemingly never-ending shale slope.

From the top, the descent didn't look too difficult. The gradient downwards was not overly steep. Once headed downwards, however, the problem became immediately apparent. The whole area was composed of shale—flat pieces of rock that had broken off and now rested on top of each other. There was no place to plant a walking stick. No flat place to put a foot. Each footstep was like stepping on a downward pointing skate board. The question wasn't how far the rock would slip, but rather whether it would slip a little or a lot. Would it stop soon enough that I could stay upright? My heart was in my throat at every step. All I could think about was that if I fell and hurt myself, it would take hours for a rescue team to get to me. And then they would have to carry me a very long distance over bad terrain. Perhaps they would drag me out on some sort of sled. My mind went around and around with disaster scenarios.

Amazingly, occasionally with a loud swoosh, a group of two or three or four bicyclists would race by. I stared at them agog. They flew over the shale, slipping and sliding but staying upright. They were going incredibly fast. If one of them lost control, went over the handle bars, landed on his head or neck, it could be lights out for good. *Why*, I wondered, *would they risk this passage instead of staying on the road?* The only thing I could think of was that it was a short-cut in relation to the road, night was coming on, and they wanted to secure a place before the hostels were all filled up. Why else take the risk? Or maybe they were thrill seekers, and this descent was talked about among bikers as a not-to-be-missed challenge. Who knew? Certainly not me, though I longed to fly over the shale as they did.

I started this descent in the middle of the afternoon. I was going so slowly that James caught up with me, and, when he saw how difficult it was for me, he kept a very slow pace alongside me. Our destination for the night was tantalizingly close. We had seen a sign a short way back that indicated we were only a couple of kilometers from our destination. Yet at each bend, all we saw was more shale. It was getting late. The light was fading. I finally asked James to scout ahead and find out how much further we had to go.

"We might end up spending the night on this mountain," I said. "It is already dangerous going down this slope. It will be even more dangerous trying to do it in the dark."

"I'll be back as soon as I can," he said, and departed.

And then I was alone. Scared. With dusk deepening, I continued inching down the slope, afraid to go on and afraid to stop.

Suddenly from behind me came a rush of sound. A group of three bicyclists roared down the shale towards me. I was thinking about diving out of the way when the lead rider put on his brakes, slipping and sliding all over the shale. The two bicyclists in his wake hit their brakes, too, and I awaited a crash of the three—but that didn't happen.

"Are you OK?" the lead rider asked me, in Italian. He wore the tradition tight Lycra bike shorts, colorful top, and pointy bicyclist helmet. *That helmet won't protect you if you go down*, I thought. He was middle aged rather than young, but incredibly fit with a lean body. The other two bicyclists were carbon copies of the leader. I noticed that their bike tires were wider than normal, probably mountain tires. *And one of these sharp shale pieces might puncture your tires.*

"I'm fine," I replied in Spanish, knowing that my white face and shaking knees and overall hunched appearance probably belied that statement.

"Do you need water?" he asked. Offering to share water is what all pilgrims do to others in distress.

"Thanks, I have water."

"Do you want one of us to stay with you?"

"Thank you, but that's not necessary. You *can* do one thing for me."

"What?"

"Down the trail somewhere, you are going to encounter a young man with very short hair and a guitar. Please tell him that you saw me and that I am OK, still descending."

"OK, we can do that. Good luck, and *Buen Camino!*" And off they sped. I sent a small prayer after them, for their safe descent.

It was almost full dark when James made it back to me.

"It's not too much farther," he said.

"We've been saying that for the last four hours," I replied, exaggerating just a bit.

"Well, it really is not too far. And then just a bit farther to our hotel."

"You went all the way to the hotel?"

"Yes. I didn't want them to give our room away to someone else, thinking we weren't coming."

"Good idea. Did you talk to some Italian bicyclists?"

"Yes, they stopped to say you were OK and coming along slowly."

Down we continued to go, at a snail's pace, step by step, feeling our way through the shale. James was with me every step.

It was nine o'clock at night before we made it to the hotel. Of all our days on the Camino, that was the latest we had ever arrived at our hotel. It was truly my worst, scariest, most unpleasant and disheartening day on the Camino.

Even so, it had its moments of grace. My son helped me. Strangers offered a random act of kindness. I made it down safely. And God answered my small prayer. I saw no broken Italian bodies on the rest of the way down.

Chapter 18
Traveling Companions

I HAD ORIGINALLY PLANNED TO WALK the Camino alone. I like solo travel. You can do exactly what you want. Get up when you want, visit what you want, eat where you want. And if you are feeling lonesome, you can always strike up a conversation with another traveler.

Admittedly, on the extrovert-introvert scale, I am decidedly an introvert. Once, in a professional group-training session, we were asked to self-identify ourselves as extroverts or introverts by going to designated ends of a room. When colleagues saw that I had placed myself among the introverts, they scoffed.

"You're no introvert," they called across the room. "Get over here!"

But I am, in fact, an introvert. At work or at business-related cocktail parties, I put on my social face and mingle. But the key is—it's *work*. Left to my own devices, I'd prefer to be at home, in bed, with a book.

Over the years, I traveled quite a bit with my mother as my traveling companion. She was more or less the opposite from me in this regard. She'd initiate a conversation with anyone, anywhere. Usually I'd just listen to what was being said, not contributing much or encouraging the contact by offering enthusiastic participation. She liked meeting new people, even if only fleetingly. I'm much more of the "why bother?" type.

I did find one useful interaction during my many years of travel. When I am with a group of strangers, particularly in a foreign country, I'll ask them, "What is the one thing you think I should see before leaving? What shouldn't I miss?" I've gotten several wonderful tips that way, leading me to seek out places I otherwise probably wouldn't have put on my visit list. For example, eating one time in a family-style restaurant in England, I asked my tablemates what they recommended. "Durham Cathedral," said one. Durham was definitely not on my itinerary up until then—but I added it, and to this day I am still recommending a visit to Durham Cathedral to anyone traveling to the north of England.

It's not that I'm totally averse to talking to strangers, just that chitchat is not for me. Solo travel usually suits me just fine.

On the other hand, traveling with a compatible companion can be wonderful. My ex-husband was a great travel partner. We liked the same things—history, art, museums, drinking sangria while reading at an outdoor café. And when something went wrong on a trip, as frequently occurs, we had the same attitude: this could have happened anywhere, so it doesn't make sense to blame the local people or the country. In the years since my divorce, I have made a number of trips with travel companions I enjoy. I have even come to appreciate the benefits of group tours, which were an anathema to me when I was younger.

But the worst, the absolute worst, *controllable* thing a traveler can do is to get yoked to an incompatible travel companion. (I say "controllable" because there are worse things that can happen, like illness or bad accidents, but those are of course not controllable.) With an incompatible travel partner, what should have been a wonderful trip will become miserable. Your travel partner will talk incessantly, whine about things that can't be helped or are just different, make poor choices, waste your precious limited time with activities that could just as well be done back at home, want to eat at McDonald's, and otherwise make you want to scream.

Due to a set of unforeseen circumstances, my son joined me on my Camino trip. A trip that I had previously thought was going to be solo totally changed in character. Perhaps because he was with me, I paid more attention than usual to other travelers and how they interacted. The Camino presented some unique challenges.

We met a lot of different combinations of travelers. Couples (both married and not), small groups, and large groups. Because of the nature of the walk, you will meet someone along the way, perhaps at breakfast or lunch, then see that person again further down the road. Recognizing a familiar face at the end of the day, perhaps someone with whom you exchanged a cheerful *"Buen Camino!"* earlier in the day, will lead you to strike up a conversation about some unusual feature or occurrence along that day's trail. This in turn opens up the opportunity for a more general conversation about your new acquaintance's overall Camino experience.

Couples. I found it interesting that, for almost all the married couples I met, there was invariably one partner who really wanted to walk the Camino, and another partner who wasn't so hot about the walking part. The enthusiastic partner wanted to walk every single step of the way. The not-so-hot partner lobbied for taking the occasional bus or taxi. Both would plead their case to third parties such as me. The enthusiastic partner would feel pressured to lessen his experience by being a slacker and cheating on the walking. The not-so-hot partner would feel pressured to walk when clearly the route was boring (and could be skipped without harming the experience), or when the day was rainy, or when one of the two was feeling ill. Ms. "No compromises" would butt heads with Mr. "This is supposed to be a vacation; let's take it easy for a day or two!"

Couples, particularly married couples, like to share life experiences such as walking the Camino. Still, I was left with the definite impression that both would have been happier if one walked the whole way, and the other arrived at the designated daily stopping place by whatever means seemed best for that particular day. They could be together each evening, sharing news of their day, but going separate ways whenever one partner didn't feel like walking. That seemed like a reasonable compromise, but I didn't come across any couples who traveled that way.

Twosomes. Non-married pairs traveling together face a different set of problems, mainly involving the actual fact of walking. People do not walk at the same pace, and invariably one person goes faster than the other. This sets up a tug-pull dynamic. The faster individual feels like he or she has to tug the other one along, while the slower walker experiences being pulled forward at a faster pace than is comfortable. As I noted above, the best solution to this seems to be for each person to walk at their own pace, and to meet up with their travel partner at a designated spot in the evening. Instead, what I usually observed was two people unwilling to split up, even when the result was resentment by one or the other.

Groups. I observed numerous groups walking the Camino, and the ones that worked the best seemed to be those in which all the members had good communication. By that I mean good cell phone coverage. The group leaders could contact stragglers, while the fast walkers could advise others of unexpected occurrences along the road. Trying to keep the group together just did not seem to work well.

What I was left with as a takeaway from observing these variously sized travel groupings is that choosing your travel companion(s) for the Camino is even more important than on a normal journey. You need to be quite clear about what you are hoping to accomplish. Is this a long-distance sprint, in order to have bragging rights? "I did the whole Camino in eighteen days!" Or do you want to stop and explore churches and museums along the way? "We spent a month on the Camino and wished we had had another week or two." If your traveling companion has a different idea about what the trip is supposed to be, you will both be unhappy.

Having decided what you want to accomplish—a marathon fast walk, or a slow exploration of the towns along the Camino, or something in between—you still have to agree on how you are going to accomplish that. Are you going to walk every last step, or are you OK with taking a bus or a taxi some days? And what if, for some reason like an illness or accident, you fall behind on your schedule? Are you going to skip ahead to catch up, or try to run the rest of the way?

How about walking style and speed? Are you fast or slow? Are you OK about walking on your own if your partner doesn't keep pace with you—or will you be annoyed with your partner for not walking fast or slow enough? A slow-burning resentment can ruin your enjoyment.

Think about attitude. Is your traveling companion generally positive or negative? Do you want to walk for a number of days with someone who complains about everything new or different or who can't understand why catsup is not available at every restaurant? Do you need a more practical companion who can point out that you really don't need that extra pound that a model of Burgos Cathedral will add to your pack? (Yes, you will be counting ounces when you are carrying your pack all day every day.)

In the case of my son and myself, almost from the very first day on the Camino my son started saying that he missed his music and wanted to buy a guitar.

"Are you nuts," I'd say. "How are you going to carry a guitar along?"

"No problem. I'm strong," he'd say.

By Burgos, I gave up and accompanied him to a guitar store, where I encouraged him to buy a small traveling guitar, rather than a full-sized model—but the one whose tone he preferred was full-sized. We left the store with a big guitar. Before we left Burgos, he had reconsidered, and he exchanged (for a fee) the full-sized guitar for a smaller one that would fit into the backpack he carried each day. He carried that guitar for the remainder of the walk and never complained about the extra weight.

I minded having to spend time on two separate days in a guitar store instead of visiting something of more interest to me, while he minded having to travel without the ability to practice his music. We worked it out, but it would have been better to have settled this before we started the trip.

Going on any trip with another person or group is always a risk, and that is even more true on the Camino. Even if you normally travel well with someone, have you taken an extended walk with him or her? If not, you might be surprised by how different and stressful walking to your destination can be. I am a slow walker, yet every day I would outpace my son by a considerable distance. He would stroll along, strumming his guitar. I would sit at our designated lunch spot, waiting for him to catch up so that we could eat and finish our walk for the day before the extreme afternoon heat hit. As long as I could hear his guitar music, or see him coming, I was fine. But when he was so far back that I could neither hear nor see him, I worried—had something happened to him? Had he taken a wrong turn? It added a stress note most days that I would have been happy to avoid.

Solo. I've been concentrating on traveling companions. But what if you decide to go alone? Isn't that dangerous? Can't you be caught somewhere with no one to help? I can understand that concern, and there were definitely some stretches along the Camino when I was glad I was not alone. (See Chapter 17, "The Worst of the Camino: Shale Hell and Boulder Purgatory," on page 81.) I wouldn't let that stop me, though. There are many, many solo walkers, and everyone along the Camino tries to help other pilgrims.

The best strategy for a solo walker is probably to stay well informed. Find out ahead of time about difficult stretches, whenever possible, and plan for those. Go around the dangerous spots via a longer but safer route if walking alone, or find someone with whom to walk. You can always team up with a partner for a day, or for a certain stretch. That happens all the time along the Camino. You decide to walk for a day or a morning with someone you have just met, with no commitment beyond that day or morning.

But even if you suddenly, unexpectedly find yourself in a bad place, you needn't despair. You can just stop and wait for someone else to come along, then ask if you can accompany them for a while. No one is going to turn you down, though they also are not going to adopt you for the rest of the walk. Once past the difficult bit, they will probably offer you a "*Buen Camino*" and speed up at their usual pace.

Should something befall you, help will come. Other walkers behind you will raise the alarm, and the *bomberos* (firemen, frequently volunteers) or other locals will evacuate you to medical assistance. The clinics and hospitals along the way are used to dealing with the accidents and foot problems that befall walkers.

My bottom line on solo traveling on the Camino is not to be afraid to try it. If it turns out not to be for you, you can probably still find a person or group along the way, or a series of people or groups along the way, with whom to tag along. They won't mind, at least for a day or two.

Of all the factors that can make your Camino wonderful or not, picking the right travel companion(s), or deciding to go it on your own, may be the most important. If you decide to go with someone, don't wait until you are there to discuss expectations and methods. The Way of St. James is going to throw up plenty of unexpected twists and turns, hills and valleys, slips and falls. At least plan for what you can, ahead of time.

Chapter 19
Modern-Day Camino Myths and Prejudices

PERHAPS UNSURPRISINGLY, there are a lot of myths and prejudices that have grown up around the Camino. The most pernicious concerns what it means to be a "real pilgrim."

Myth No. 1: A true pilgrim walks the whole way.

According to the Catholic Church—the ultimate earthly authority on the issue of who qualifies—anyone who walks the last 100 kilometers into Santiago de Compostela, or who bikes or rides a horse the last 200 kilometers, is a bona fide pilgrim entitled to receive the Compostela, the Church's certificate given to pilgrims who apply for it at the end of their journey.

But along the way, you will hear almost all modern-day pilgrims spouting off about who is a "true *peregrino*."

The strongest purists believe that a pilgrim must walk every single step of the way, carrying all of his or her gear on his or her back. Anyone else is cheating.

Bicyclists, no matter how far they pedal, are cheating.

The few horseback riders are cheating.

Anyone who sends their backpacks ahead with the companies who provide this service is cheating.

Those who stay anywhere other than a pilgrim hostel every night of the trip are cheating.

Anyone who takes a bus, taxi, or other wheeled mode of transport, for whatever reason, is cheating.

This attitude pushes people, who might otherwise choose *not* to walk every step, to do so, backpacks weighing down each step during the day. At night, this attitude compels some travelers to sleep in dormitory rooms with forty other snoring people, even though they sorely need undisturbed sleep.

From the absolute purist at the top, there are a number of gradations on down as to what is considered acceptable, and what is not, depending upon the person who is doing the judging. Obviously, for the numerous bicyclists, biking is fine. For the many, many people who hire a service to hump their backpacks forward, that is fine.

The only red line seems to be the Church's. You can't get your Compostela unless you have walked that last 100 kilometers, and documented it. I am still unsure why the last 100 kilometers qualify a pilgrim, but not the first 100, or any 100 in the middle—but those are the rules. The result is that the most crowded part of the Camino is the last 100 kilometers, and many people join the Camino at Sarria just to be sure they can get their Compostela.

Leaving the Church rules aside, let's consider what a pilgrim in the Middle Ages did. Those pilgrims of former times, if they had the means, rode to Compostela, either on horseback or in a wheeled vehicle. They presumably carried very little, like modern-day pilgrims, but whatever their baggage was, if they could afford it, that baggage would be conveyed on a pack horse or in a cart. Those olden-day pilgrims went the whole way from their starting point, wherever that was, and then they turned around (if they were still alive) and went all the way back home by the same means. It was always a two-way journey by foot or horseback or cart.

In my whole Camino, I only encountered three pilgrims going in the opposite direction—returning home by the same means they had gone to Santiago de Compostela. Almost everyone flies home, if they come from far away, or otherwise goes home by train or bus.

When I would overhear a purist make a snide remark about another traveler cheating, I would pipe up and ask, "Are you planning to walk home?" No one ever responded "yes," or even for that matter seemed to understand what I was getting at.

Before I left for the Camino, I attended many gatherings of the local Houston APOC chapter, and was the recipient of a lot of good advice from my Camino mentor and other members of the chapter. A frequent phrase I'd hear was, "It's your Camino," meaning the Camino is whatever you want it to be, whatever you design it to be. Obviously, that is true. Each of us decides how we will travel.

Nevertheless, running into those who talk about "cheating" and "true pilgrims" and hearing those nasty comments about others is a daily occurrence on the Camino. I was really surprised and shocked by how un-Christian so many pilgrims seemed to be. Instead of respecting everyone for at least *attempting* this difficult challenge and for undertaking the Camino at the level of difficulty the person thought he could manage, those self-declared "true pilgrims" seemed to want to hog the "pilgrim" designation only for themselves and others like them who adhered to some arbitrary set of standards.

Perhaps it is these self-appointed judges who inspired the many aphorisms one encounters along the Way, such as, "It is not the destination, but the journey." Based on my experience, all of us need those reminders.

Myth No. 2: The Camino is a pilgrimage.

My *American Heritage Dictionary* defines a "pilgrim" as a "religious devotee who journeys to a shrine or sacred place" or as someone "who embarks on a quest for some end conceived as sacred." (As a third definition, *American Heritage* throws in "any traveler." For that third definition, I can't help but hear John Wayne labeling naïve travelers as "pilgrims.") As for a pilgrimage, the dictionary says that it is a "journey to a sacred place or shrine" or any "long journey or search, especially one of exalted purpose or moral significance." These principal definitions all include an element of religion or sacredness.

Maybe in the Middle Ages the Camino was truly a pilgrimage for most, though I have my doubts about that too. (Reading Chaucer's *Canterbury Tales*, one gets an idea of the range of motivating factors for a pilgrimage.) Nowadays, if you go on the Camino thinking you are on a pilgrimage in the sense of a journey with an element of religion or sacredness, you are going to be in lonely company.

I found it eye-opening to see the number of Asians, particularly Koreans, walking the Camino. Why, I wondered, would Asians be attracted to a centuries-old Christian pilgrimage route? The answer of course, is that the Camino is no longer truly a pilgrimage. It is Europe's long walk, the equivalent of our Appalachian or Pacific Coast trails. The religious or sacred element has been largely removed from the Camino, both by the travelers themselves and by the fact that so few churches are open to visit.

While walking, I only encountered two couples traveling together who were saying their rosary as they progressed along. I had the opportunity to chat with this group at a rest stop and learned that they had been motivated by hearing about the Camino at their Catholic church back home in New Orleans.

I met another woman—only one—who was giving away plastic rosaries. To her, I displayed my own lack of charity. "I can't believe," I said, "how few people seem to view this as a pilgrimage. They don't pray. They don't visit churches. Their only goal seems to be to walk as fast as possible from one point to another." She chided me: "We all have our own reasons for walking."

I also observed a group of high schoolers stopped at a closed chapel, being led in prayer by a priest. Clearly the group was on a religious trip organized by their school, but unluckily for them the chapel they were visiting wasn't open, so they had to say their devotions on foot, in the road.

The only other examples of religiosity I saw were the "pilgrim's masses" held at some of the larger churches along the Camino. The pilgrim's mass at Roncesvalles drew a large crowd, and I observed a good-sized number of *peregrinos* at a few other pilgrim's masses. At the end of these specially designated masses, pilgrims are usually invited up to the front of the church and asked to tell congregants where they come from. Sometimes the priest leads the pilgrims in a special song (which all the Spanish know, but not the foreign pilgrims), and usually the priest gives the pilgrims a special blessing after reading a prayer to St. James or something similar.

It is also fairly common for the priest to say words of welcome to the pilgrims and to offer them encouragement on the journey. In those cases, a bilingual Spanish-English speaker is asked to volunteer to translate the priest's remarks, for the benefit of those pilgrims who do not speak Spanish. I performed that service at one mass.

These pilgrim's masses seemed to be offered more frequently on Sunday, as could be expected. If a pilgrim sets out thinking she can attend mass every morning along the Camino, I am afraid she will be sorely disappointed. There are too many villages whose churches are closed most days of the week.

I unfortunately missed the religious ceremony in Santiago de Compostela which is the most talked about—and which I most wished to attend—the swinging down the main cathedral aisle of a massive thurible (a metal censor suspended on chains). The thurible emits a cloud of incense as it slices by on its long arc. Priests have to manage the passage of the huge vessel, raising and lowering it as necessary to accomplish the arc. This ceremony is only offered occasionally, and not on any set schedule. I was in Santiago for three days at the end of my walk, but the Botafumeiro, as this famous thurible is known, did not swing on any of those three days.

It is considered rude while on the Camino directly to ask someone why he is walking, though many pilgrims will volunteer their reasons. Few who spoke about it cited spiritual reasons. Some said it was a challenge, or their friend had done it and it sounded like a fun thing to do. Others said they wanted to find themselves or re-evaluate their lives, which of course can have a spiritual component but can also be totally devoid of thinking about God and one's path in terms of sin and redemption.

I was also shocked and dismayed at how many churches along the route were locked up tight, except perhaps on Sunday and, even then, only open for a few hours. My own resolution along the Camino quickly became "Never pass up an open church," and I made it my habit always to thank the volunteers who were staffing the open churches and also to make a small donation. I am sorry to say that most pilgrims raced by those open churches without stopping to offer a brief prayer or to take a quick look at these medieval remnants of faith, charity, architecture, and art.

Myth No. 3: Spain is proud of the Camino and acts like it.

Unfortunately, this is truly a myth. I'd say that Spaniards are proud of the Camino, and by their actions are hospitable and welcoming. Spain, however, as a government, seems to put little value in the Camino. During our whole walk, I only came across one place where a Spanish road crew was working to improve the path. Most efforts to maintain the Way seem to be funded by volunteer groups, especially international volunteer groups. The Camino could desperately use more shade trees along certain places (like the Meseta), benches for tired pilgrims to rest briefly, water fountains, trash cans that are not overflowing with smelly contents, and road signs. Perhaps someone somewhere thinks that the Camino should remain rough and primitive, that part of its purpose is to make us suffer. Pain as prayer. But I encountered places that were truly dangerous, and I can't understand the government not wanting to eliminate those. Walking for hundreds of kilometers is hard enough in itself, without having the paths be slippery, rocky, and treacherous.

Nor does the government of Spain invest resources to help the Spanish people living in the northern areas or the pilgrims visiting there. There were many towns with no bus service whatsoever. You couldn't get from one town to another except by walking or by hiring a taxi or private car to take you. I would always ask about this, and the locals would respond that there used to be a bus but that it had been discontinued. I kept thinking that was a penny-wise, pound-foolish governmental decision.

Pilgrims have brought an economic boom to the villages and towns along the Way, with signs of economic revival everywhere evident as a result of the recent large influxes of pilgrims. New B&Bs, hostels, and cafés are springing up in what were previously essentially ghost towns. The pilgrims are breathing new life into these villages. Given a secure, inexpensive, more reliable mode of transportation, such as a regularly scheduled bus line all along the Camino, even more pilgrims might venture to try the Camino, by bus if not on foot.

Myth No. 4: The Camino is for the young.

There are a lot of young people walking the Camino. You will see everything from high school groups to gangs of college-aged kids. But you will also see quite a large number of older folks. After all, like me, it is only in retirement that most of us have the time and resources to make an extended visit to a foreign country. I saw many people older than me on the Camino, almost all of whom left me in the dust in terms of speed of walking.

* * *

These are four of the myths I encountered as I prepared for and then experienced the Camino. I would like to drive a stake in the heart of the "true pilgrim" rubbish and hope that this chapter goes at least a short way towards accomplishing that purpose. I would also like to encourage Camino walkers to add churches to their itineraries, for aesthetic and historical if not spiritual reasons. In another chapter, I will be advocating for the Government of Spain to spend more resources on its precious jewel, the Camino. Finally, I hope my advice helps senior citizens realize that, yes, you can do the Camino. If this book helps to accomplish any of these purposes, I will feel that I have given back in a small measure to the Way.

Chapter 20
Alternate Ways Besides Walking

I N THE PREVIOUS CHAPTER, I outlined some of the culture of the Camino, including myths and prejudices. Those myths and prejudices influence how a pilgrim experiences the Camino.

The dominant Camino culture is definitely to walk—and only walk—the path towards Santiago de Compostela. There are dedicated Camino enthusiasts who have walked to Santiago many times, usually trying out different routes. One year those pilgrims will walk the French route, then the next year the Portuguese route. Or the Coastal route. Or the *Primitivo* (primitive) route. There are so many different ways to get to Santiago, depending upon your starting point, that walkers can vary their route year after year for many years.

For those who can't take a vacation long enough to walk a whole route, some pilgrims will break up their trip into segments and walk one or more *stages* one year, then another segment the following year. So, for example, maybe their first walk will be from Saint-Jean-Pied-de-Port on the French side of the Pyrenees to Burgos, and then the next year they will continue their journey by going from Burgos to León, and so forth.

Walkers, particularly those who stay exclusively in hostels, have their own subculture. Walkers wake up and depart from their lodgings very, very early, with the hostels usually requiring that early departure. This system allows those who run the hostels to clean and prepare the premises for the next batch of walkers, many of whom will arrive in the early afternoon. Some hostels fill up very early—like 2:00 pm—so if a pilgrim wants to secure a hostel bed for the next night, he has to get to the next place as soon as possible. This time imperative partially accounts for the pilgrims who dash past beautiful ancient churches along the route with nary a peek inside. They have to make it to the next stopping point in time to claim a bed for the night.

Others, like myself, are more relaxed about walking and do a mix of walking and taking public transportation. Having heard from my Camino mentor Julia Wagener about the possibilities of getting injured while walking, I never told people, when talking about the Camino before departure, that I planned to walk the whole route. I said that I would walk what I could.

That cautious approach turned out to be a fortunate decision, because my son decided to join me on the walk but then developed plantar fasciitis along the way and was unable to walk. A mixed journey became a necessity. Some days we would catch a bus to the next stopping place. Sometimes there was no bus available, so we would take a taxi to the next town. Sometimes he took public transportation while I walked, in which case we met up at night at our lodging place. We decided how to move forward each day, as we went along, based on public transportation options and the route for the day. If I could avoid a steep hill by going along with my son on a particular day, public transportation won out. (My elevation map of the *stages*, acquired at the Pilgrim Office in Saint-Jean-Pied-de-Port, became something I consulted each and every day before deciding whether I would walk or ride.)

One caution about this mixed approach to traveling the Camino: it is difficult if not impossible to put together a trip exclusively by bus. There are unfortunately many small towns that are not connected by any public transportation other than taxis. If you want to travel the way James did—by public transportation, stopping at small towns and villages and not just zooming from big city to big city—you have to be willing to take a taxi to your next stop whenever a bus is not available. Luckily, the taxi charges are reasonable.

At bus stops, we ran into all sorts of other pilgrims. Most seemed to be walkers who, for one reason or another, couldn't walk on a particular day. I met a heavily pregnant woman, who looked like she was going to be dropping her baby any day. She told me she and her husband were walking the Camino, but she needed to rest on that day. I was amazed that her family and doctor had allowed her to undertake this strenuous journey in her last month of pregnancy. I said a prayer for her, asking that she receive the Virgin's help to make it home before the birth. (A prayerful appeal like this one seemed best addressed to the Virgin Mary, who herself had had to make a long and difficult journey while heavily pregnant.)

Other bus riders had various sorts of injuries. Some volunteered that their time was running out and that they needed to speed up their journey in order to get to Santiago to catch their plane home. Still others said they had already walked a particular stretch and wanted to hop over it to the next part, or that they didn't fancy walking the Meseta, or that they had decided to spend an extra night in one stopping place and now had to make up time to stay on schedule or to catch up with their friends.

There were many valid reasons for catching the bus, but all, and I mean all, of those waiting for the bus who exchanged information seemed to be apologizing for having to take the bus. Their words and tone of voice clearly signaled that they judged that they had failed, that they had not met the demands of the pilgrimage. In short, they had bought into the myth that true pilgrims only walked.

Balderdash! I say. As I have pointed out elsewhere, medieval pilgrims got to Compostela as best they could. Those who could afford it rode horseback. James Michener, who inspired me to experience the Camino, himself only walked a short segment, as far as I can determine from his chapter on the Camino in *Iberia*, yet he conveyed in that chapter the mystery and romance and spirituality of the Camino better than so many others have. I wanted to travel the

Camino like Michener had done it, taking in the history and beauty and culture of the places I passed through rather than just slogging along from one town to another as rapidly as possible.

Something that appealed to me—and which I explored a bit before abandoning the idea—was to go on the Camino by horseback. Now *that* option would be traveling the pilgrimage route the way so many long-ago pilgrims had experienced it. There is at least one group tour that you can sign up for that will get you to Santiago by horseback, with the required (for the Compostela) 200 kilometers under your horse's hooves. The downside that I saw to such horseback tours was that, in order to complete the journey in a reasonable amount of time, the tour requires very long days in the saddle and doesn't give much if any time for savoring the places along the way.

Bicycling the Camino is another, quite popular option. The bikers by and large stay at the hostels, and they seem to travel in packs. I did meet one family group traveling by bike, and the parents proudly boasted of how many kilometers their youngest child, perhaps eight years old, had been able to complete in a day. Biking looked to me to be a reasonable, and faster, alternative to walking. The downside, of course, is that bikers keep to roads and hence do not travel along the narrow stone or dirt paths that most pilgrims use. I saw bikers load and unload their bikes onto buses, so a mixed bike-public transport option is also a possibility.

Whenever I came to a paved downward incline, I longed for a bike or even a skateboard so that I could speed downhill on glorious wheels with minimum effort. There are a few places along the Camino that rent bikes. While I seriously thought a time or two about renting a bike, in the end I never did so.

Surprisingly, I did not see many commercial tour groups along the Camino. Maybe I just did not run into them, but the market is dominated by walkers.

Everyone has to make her own decision about how to carry out her Camino journey in a meaningful way, but I highly recommend the Michener approach. While I used the mixed approach myself, and thoroughly enjoyed the trip, if I were to do the Camino a second time, I would rent a car and drive the Camino. For me, actually walking the Camino is not as important as experiencing it, drinking it all in—the art, the history, the religiosity that guided and formed the lives of those long-ago pilgrims. I want to *savor* it, not suffer through it. I want that feeling of being close to something greater than myself when I sit quietly and look at a luminous stained-glass window.

Others will disagree. For them, the long stretches of walking, when one is almost forced to think about the status of one's life, are purifying and provide a true pilgrim experience. For me, my thoughts usually seemed to be along the lines of "How much farther do I have to walk before I can finally eat lunch?" or something equally unspiritual. My spiritual experiences came as I wandered through a ruined church, or sat quietly in a church and thought about those who had worshipped there.

Like Michener, I do think all pilgrims should walk a stretch or two, at least, just to experience the on-foot pilgrim journey. How to manage that in a rental car is a bit of a puzzle, but not insurmountable. One way could be to walk an occasional stretch between two towns that are connected by a bus route, so that you could catch the bus back to where your rental car is parked, or some variation of that. Another, even more appealing approach would be to travel your Camino with a friend or friends. On any given day, one or more pilgrims in the group could walk while a designated driver moved the car forward to the next stop. And then for another stretch, the designated driver could change.

No matter what you decide, I urge you to stay flexible. Don't pin all your hopes and dreams for the trip on walking the whole way in a certain amount of time. If you do, you might end up disappointed when injury or circumstances intervene. Better, I think, is to place the whole issue in the hands of the Saint and say, "I plan to walk as much as I can and hope to offer a prayer of thanks to St. James in Santiago for a successful journey, however much I end up walking." *Buen Camino!*

Chapter 21
Father Elías Valiña

IN OUR LIFETIMES, WE ARE PRIVILEGED to watch a few people that we can all recognize as "saints"—people who live a saintly life, who put others before themselves, who offer a service to mankind. People like Mother Teresa spring to mind when we think of modern-day saints. During the Middle Ages, a surprisingly large number of saints gained their sainthood thanks to services they offered to pilgrims along the Camino.

I know nothing about the private life of Father Elías Valiña. In his private life, he might have been the most horrendous person, guilty of the worst sins, a brother to so many of the modern-day clergy, as the recent scandals of the Catholic Church are revealing. Instead, I base my belief in his merits for sainthood not on his private life, but on his public life, and on what he gave back to the world.

In my own spiritual garden, I have awarded sainthood to three persons. The first of these is my sister, who was struck down at twelve years of age with a horrible disease that left her unable to function independently, or to grow intellectually past the age of a two-year-old. By all of the measures of the Catholic Church, she qualifies for sainthood. She was baptized, confirmed, and followed the dictates of the Church until the terrible sword descended on her life. She never really had a chance to become a sinner. When I pray, I usually bring Saint Muffet into the prayer.

I also consider my mother a saint because, for all of her flaws and faults, she undertook the care of my sister without complaint for forty years. She lived her penance on earth.

And I count Father Elías Valiña as my third saint.

Father Elías took a moribund institution, the pilgrimage route to Santiago de Compostela, and breathed new life into it. He traveled in his trusty Deux Chevaux automobile throughout Spain, his can of yellow paint and paint brush handy. He stopped at intersections and painted bright yellow arrows. He went to conferences, national and international, and shared his knowledge about the Camino with learned men and women throughout the world.

Curiosity about the yellow arrows, and academic interest in the Camino, began to grow. From a tiny trickle of pilgrims in the late 1950s, the number of people converging on Santiago de Compostela has now swollen to more than half a million annually, according to the figures kept by the Catholic Church.

While I walked the Camino, I thought about Father Elías a lot. He seemed to me rather a modern-day Don Quijote, tilting at the windmill of lost memory about the Camino. In one of the small hotels at which I stayed, I came across an article in Spanish about him, and learned something more about his life than I had previously known. When I reached O'Cebreiro, I went into the garden that holds markers from many countries, stones and plaques from national groups memorializing Father Elías for having revived the Camino movement. I was dismayed to find no marker from APOC, so I went into the church office to enquire. No, I was told, I was not mistaken. There was no marker from the American pilgrims. I asked the lady staffing the desk if such a plaque or stone would be welcomed. "Certainly," she said, "we have them from around the world."

I then launched my own quixotic effort to get American thanks to Father Elías added to the collection. I emailed APOC and my local chapter leaders, I posted notes on various blogs and Facebook sites, I talked to other pilgrims. My efforts ended fruitlessly, as I was told that no more plaques could be added to the garden, though that is not what I had been told at O'Cebreiro. I still regret that APOC has not made an effort to honor Father Valiña in some way.

What a pity that this modern-day saint, who launched this massive re-awakening that has brought so much joy and adventure and spiritual growth to so many, is not more recognized and praised and taken as a model. If a can of yellow paint can turn a trickle into a torrent, what could we each do in our own lives to turn things around, to bring back the best of the past and make it work in today's world?

For the Catholic Church, proof of sainthood is demonstrated by miracles attributable to the proposed saint. Father Elías's miracle was to revive the Camino, and to give it to the rest of us. May Saint Elías guide us, on our journey on the Camino, and through life.

Chapter 22
The Compostela

ONE DECISION YOU HAVE TO MAKE is whether you care about getting a Compostela at the end of your journey. That decision will affect your planning for the trip.

The Compostela is a certificate, given to you by the Catholic Church in Santiago de Compostela, that certifies that you have made a pilgrimage to Santiago. It is a beautiful document, written in Latin, and perfect for framing and hanging on your wall. It gives you permanent bragging rights about having completed the Camino de Santiago.

The minimum requirement for getting the Compostela is to walk the last 100 kilometers along the Camino. The catch is that the only place the Compostela is given out is in Santiago, so you have to end your journey there to get it. That practical aspect, coupled with the fact that most pilgrims want to see Santiago de Compostela, means that the last 100 kilometers of the French route are the most traveled section of the Camino.

In order to prove that you have in fact walked the necessary distance, you have to have your Camino "passport" (also called a credential, or *credencial* in Spanish) stamped at least twice a day during that last 100 kilometers. Camino passports can be obtained at tourist offices along the route, or ordered in advance of your trip from organizations like APOC.

Hotels, restaurants, bars—most public places catering to tourists and pilgrims along the Way—have a rubber stamp and an ink pad at the ready for you. Most of those places have stamps that just give the name of the location and the town and leave room for the date, but some of the stamps are unusual or unique. Pilgrims show off those special stamps to others. Some places stamp your passport, while others just leave a stamp and ink pad out on a counter or desk and invite you to stamp your own passport. There is no charge for a stamp.

A short digression on churches in Spain. Although Spain is renowned as being a very Catholic country, religion seems in decline there. The number of closed churches along the Camino is disheartening. To be able to visit a church, you have to be there at the right time, such as when a mass is scheduled, or else the doors will be firmly locked. Given that the stealing of sacred art and artifacts is a booming business, I suppose locking up churches tight is justified. But if you are making the pilgrimage for religious reasons, it is very disappointing to see so many churches, particularly in small towns, closed. In one town, I went back to a church several times in an attempt to catch it open, but I never succeeded.

Not too long into our walk, I made a decision to stop in at *every* church that I saw was open along the route. It wasn't as many as you might think. If the church was open, usually there was someone there to show you around the church, if you desired it, and to talk with you about the church, the saint for which it was named, the town, the Camino, or whatever else was on your mind—and, of course, to stamp your Camino passport. (Not all churches had a stamp, but most did.)

I always tried to get a stamp from the churches I visited. I also made a small donation to the church to cover the costs of keeping the church open and staffing it with someone who could answer my questions. I made it a point to thank the person in the church for opening it so that pilgrims could stop in. Having a religious stamp in my passport seemed more fitting than a bar's, but I always took what I could get, and sweated when I left a place and forgot to ask for a stamp.

At one of the churches, I met a gentleman who told me that he was a member of a Catholic organization that had taken as one of its missions the staffing of churches along the Camino. (The group's main purpose was to serve as lay missionaries in Africa and Latin America.) Members of that group were, by serving in Spain, in effect being missionaries in their own country. Certainly, they were offering a service that I appreciated. (See Chapter 23, "A Day-by-Day Journal of the Trip," on page 115, for more on this organization.)

Back to the Compostela. When you go to get your Compostela, your Camino passport is examined for the requisite stamps. If you present adequate documentation, you can also have the Compostela show the full distance in kilometers that you have walked. In my case, I had completely filled one passport with stamps about half-way through my journey and then started on a second passport.

Because I only needed to demonstrate the last 100 kilometers, and because I didn't know about the option to have the total kilometers noted on the Compostela, I didn't bother to take the first passport with me to the Compostela office. The staffer told me that I could come back another day with both passports and get a Compostela showing the full distance I had walked—of course for a second fee—but in the end I didn't bother going back. I had a Compostela, which is all I really wanted.

My son was very doubtful about whether he cared about getting a Compostela. *Why bother?* he wondered. Many don't take the time to go to the necessary office, pay the fee, wait in line to be questioned in order to be approved for the Compostela, and wait again to receive it. Repeat pilgrims who already have a Compostela often don't bother to get another one.

In truth, I believe the rules about the Compostela should be revised and updated. It seems to me that walking any 100 kilometers along the route should qualify, not just the last 100 kilometers. There should be a way to send in your passport electronically and receive your Compostela by mail.

After all, the Compostela is not really worth anything, except to the person who has earned it (as is true for a graduation diploma, for example). You can't use it to get a job, or even to impress a girl (or at least not most girls). So why not be more generous in giving them out to pilgrims who, for one reason or another—ranging from running out of funds or time to getting injured—can't walk the last 100 kilometers into Santiago? They may have walked more than the 100 kilometers required on an earlier *stage* of the Camino, but can't walk the last 100 kilometers into Santiago.

I read, proudly and happily, that the Church had given a Compostela to the parents of a girl who some years ago was murdered as she was walking the Camino. The Church of course was right to give her parents her Compostela, and in my opinion they should also give out Compostelas more generously to others.

A decision on whether or not you prize the receipt of a Compostela will shape your journey. Depending on how much time and money you have, it will determine where you start your Camino.

Chapter 23
A Day-by-Day Journal of the Trip

B EFORE I STARTED THE CAMINO, I decided that I would write a blog along the way. Blogs and blogging were new to me, but I thought it might be an interesting experience. I have kept travel journals, in a haphazard way, for years.

In my journals, I kept track of not just what I did on particular days, but also of expenses and purchases. I thought that blogging might offer certain advantages, like giving me a record of the trip into which I could integrate photographs. It would let me create a travel document I could share in real time with family and friends back home. I resolved to take more photographs than I usually do, and to select one emblematic photo for each day.

All of what I had thought about the advantages of blogging was true, but what I didn't anticipate was the difficulty of using the necessary technology to support a blog while in northern Spain. Uploading was a major problem in many places, and it seemed as if I were wasting hours each day struggling with the technology instead of experiencing the journey.

Towards the end of the trip I gave up the blogging and went back to journaling, again in a haphazard way, by which I mean I am not very strict with myself about writing each day. Rather, sometimes I will let the journal go for several days and then catch up. The entries below will be a mix of my blog and, at the end, my journal.

In writing this book, I took a few of the events I wrote about on my blog, like meeting The Truffle Hunter, and expanded the entry into a chapter for this book. In such instances, I have deleted the relevant portions of the blog entries below to avoid redundancy. I have also slightly edited some blog entries.

You will read in these entries references to photographs that do not appear in this book. If you wish to see those photographs, you can see them on my blog, Camino for Boomers:

CaminoforBoomers.com

As part of the publication of this book, I plan to go back to my blog and rework it, adding journal entries for the final days of the trip as well as a lot more color photographs. I urge you to visit the blog as a way to see more photographs of the interesting and unusual sights we saw along the Camino.

My guest bedroom became the place to test out my packing plans. I added and subtracted items until I thought I had included the necessary but eliminated the superfluous.

James's back and daypacks ready to go!

Getting Ready to Go
Wednesday, May 25, 2016
Houston, Texas
Camino Day Minus 7

James and I have been getting ready to go on our great Camino de Santiago adventure for weeks. James already has his clothes in his backpack. My clothes have been in and out of my suitcase several times, as I add and discard items and weigh the results. Fifty pounds is the max.

I have contracted with Camino Ways, a company that will move my suitcase and his large backpack as necessary to the next hotel as we walk the Camino. James would like to schlep all his stuff himself, but not me!

So Many Books, So Few Pounds Available
Saturday, May 28, 2016
Houston, Texas
Camino Day Minus 4

Starting this blog is an experiment; it's my first blog, and I'm not at all sure what I am doing. When I scheduled my walk on the Camino, I thought I would be walking alone. I tried to think about what could set my blog apart from other blogs and other books on the Camino. I knew I was not going to be a "hard-core" pilgrim.

At my age, and with my compromised health, I needed to be a bit forgiving to my body. I thought a blog focused on walking the easy way might be useful and interesting. Hence, I named my blog "Camino for Boomers."

Since that decision, my son James, twenty-four years old, has decided to walk with me. He is going to participate in the walk and in the blog, so suddenly the name of the blog is not quite so accurate. Except, maybe his participation has given me my first tip for Boomers: If you can arrange to walk with a younger person, even for a portion of the walk, do it.

James has already helped with a number of aspects of preparing for the trip. He has packed safety items and a medical kit. And maybe he'll even carry a book or two for me.

SIGNS, OMENS, PORTENTS
SUNDAY, MAY 29, 2016
HOUSTON, TEXAS
CAMINO DAY MINUS 3

I had originally planned to take this trip in 2014, as my first major trip after retiring. Cancer intervened, so I postponed.

This past winter I finally felt well enough to reschedule the walk. I had an itinerary and reservations and everything. Then a family imbroglio erupted, and I was forced to postpone again.

Next, I found out that my copy of *Iberia* had gone walkabout—sort of fitting, in a funny way.

I was forced to ponder whether God, or fate, or the stars perhaps didn't want me to take the trip. Maybe I was stubbornly ignoring the signs and trying to force my will about what should be. I had learned quite early in my life that, despite what we are taught and believe, we are not masters of our own fate; things happen over which we have no control.

Then this past Tuesday I went out to lunch at a Chinese restaurant. I almost never eat the fortune cookie, but this time I did. My fortune: "Only those who dare truly live." Finally, a sign telling me to carry on.

LAST DRINKS IN THE USA, OR, JAMES SAVED THE DAY
SUNDAY, MAY 29, 2016
HOUSTON, TEXAS, TO WASHINGTON, DC, TO MADRID
CAMINO DAY MINUS 3 (CONTINUED)

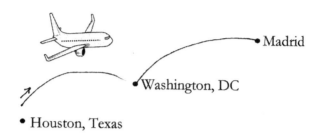

I had planned to take a picture of us outside my front door with
our suitcases as we got ready to leave on our pilgrimage. But we were
too rushed, so instead you are seeing a photo of our last drinks in the
USA before we boarded the plane to Spain. James with his Blue Moon
including orange slice and me with my plain Jane Miller Light.

James deserved the premium beer. He saved the day this morning. Our Super Shuttle (also known as the Blue Van) driver left without
us after waiting for us maybe a minute. I was freaking out. I was having no luck with booking another driver or a taxi. It was Memorial
Day weekend, after all. Parking at the airport for the duration of this
long trip would be outrageously expensive.

James suggested Uber. The Uber guy arrived in six minutes and
was fabulous. We made it to the airport with time to spare. I made a
vow never again to use the Super Shuttle; Uber will be just fine.
Hooray for Uber (my first Uber ride) and James! And bottoms up to
the Camino!

YES, WE DRANK THE WHOLE THING
MONDAY, MAY 30, 2016
MADRID TO SORIA TO PAMPLONA
CAMINO DAY MINUS 2

Our first night in Spain, in fact our first night on the trip, and we were tired after following up the flight to Madrid with a bus ride to Pamplona. Our plane routing is Houston to Madrid, and from Madrid we have to make our way to Saint-Jean-Pied-de-Port to start our Camino. We booked a bus to Pamplona, and tomorrow we will take a second bus from Pamplona to Saint-Jean-Pied-de-Port.

After checking in at our hotel, we took a nap. Then up and out for dinner. Thank goodness the Spanish eat late. We found a nice neighborhood restaurant with a menu of the day that came with wine, beer, or bottled water. James asked for beer, but I went for the wine. The waiter brought a full bottle of a Navarrese wine.

I asked, "Am I supposed to have a glass of this?"

He replied, "The bottle comes with the meal."

So, yes, we drank the whole thing. James helped. The best sleep aid possible for two jet-lagged pilgrims.

ST. JAMES THE PILGRIM
TUESDAY, MAY 31, 2016
PAMPLONA TO SAINT-JEAN-PIED-DE-PORT
CAMINO DAY MINUS 1

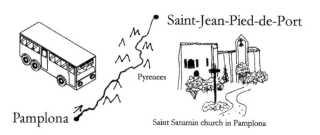

Saint-Jean-Pied-de-Port

Pyrenees

Pamplona

Saint Saturnin church in Pamplona

In Pamplona this morning, we visited Saint Saturnin Church. Saint Saturnin proselytized in Pamplona and converted the first Christians there. He was later martyred. The statue of St James the Pilgrim is one of many beautiful statues in the church, including one of Mary, the Virgin of the Camino, dating from 1487.

10,749 STEPS TODAY

The author and her son outside the Pilgrims Office in
Saint-Jean-Pied-de-Port, where they collected some very useful
documents, including an elevation map that they used throughout
their trip. They also got their first stamp in their Camino passports!

AND WE'RE OFF!
WEDNESDAY, JUNE 1, 2016
SAINT-JEAN-PIED-DE-PORT, FRANCE, TO VALCARLOS, SPAIN
DAY 1

In James Michener 's *Iberia*, he says that all medieval pilgrims had four essential items: a warm cloak that could also be used as a blanket or pillow; an eight-foot staff for walking and for keeping off aggressive dogs, spangled with gourds holding wine or water; sturdy sandals; and a wide-brimmed floppy hat.

As we set off on our journey from Saint-Jean-Pied-de-Port, we are not that different from those earlier pilgrims. We have our impermeable jackets on or strapped to our backpacks. Our walking sticks, while not eight feet tall, are fairly tall. Instead of gourds we have fancy new hydration packs, but they serve the same purpose as the gourds.

We spent a lot of time trying to locate the right, sturdy but comfortable, hiking boots. And we both have our hats. Mine is wide brimmed. James's can more correctly be deemed "jaunty." You'll see it in a future post. And, of course, we both carry our cockleshells, mine affixed to my backpack.

A staffer at the Pilgrim's Office kindly took this photo of us.

This was a very rough day for me. More steps than ever, many of them uphill. I was ready to quit two-thirds of the way to Valcarlos, but James urged me on. I finally straggled in quite late.

27,175 STEPS TODAY

RONCESVALLES MEANS CHARLEMAGNE, ROLAND,
   AND SANCHO THE STRONG
THURSDAY, JUNE 2, 2016
VALCARLOS TO RONCESVALLES
DAY 2

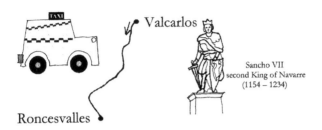

Valcarlos

Roncesvalles

Sancho VII
second King of Navarre
(1154 – 1234)

In Roncesvalles, history comes alive. This is where Roland, of the famous *Song of Roland*, fought his last battle for Charlemagne and died. Here too 7'2" King Sancho the Strong of Navarre, who battled to expel the Moors from Spain, is buried. It's a tiny town but packed with history.

I woke up this morning with an arm swollen from lymphedema, a legacy of my cancer surgery. That means no more weight on my shoulder, no more carrying a backpack for a while. I also doubted whether I could have made the steep climb up the mountain. We rode a taxi in comfort from Valcarlos to Roncesvalles and spent the day exploring the town.

11,242 STEPS TODAY

Although this looks like a fairly flat surface, in fact it is a decline, and an extremely slippery one at that, due to the rocks, small stones, and shale underfoot. Trying to make my way on this surface made this the worst hiking day of the trip. I believe that the government of Spain should fix dangerous stretches of the Camino like this one.

WALKING THE WALK
FRIDAY, JUNE 3, 2016
RONCESVALLES TO ZUBIRI
DAY 3

This day was walking, all day. Twelve hours of walking. Much too ambitious a day for me.

I was ready to call it quits at about 3:00 pm, but James wanted to continue, so we did. The last descent was steep, over shale that was slippery and super dangerous. The photo is an optical illusion, making the path look basically flat. In fact, the path was mostly downhill, which added to its slipperiness.

I only hoped to get to Zubiri by nightfall, and we did, around 9 pm. An amazing number of steps for me. I usually only walk around 5,000 steps on an average day.

49,806 STEPS TODAY

RETURN TO PAMPLONA
SATURDAY, JUNE 4, 2016
ZUBIRI TO PAMPLONA
DAY 4

Zubiri

Pamplona

Ernest Hemingway
(1899 – 1961)

Pamplona of course was one of the, if not the, favorite places of
Ernest Hemingway. You find traces of him all over town—his favorite hotel, his favorite bar, his favorite.... It was fun catching up
with him late at night in one of his favorite bars.

After our brutal walk from Roncesvalles to Zubiri, we decided to
take the bus to Pamplona. At the bus stop we met a number of other
pilgrims who were also ready for a ride rather than a walk.

We had stopped overnight in Pamplona on our journey from
Madrid to Saint-Jean-Pied-de-Port, but had had time only to visit the
Church of St. Saturnin. Before we could explore more of Pamplona,
we had housekeeping to do—laundry. After that, we went to a club
to hear a Spanish singer-songwriter, Pablo Carbonell. Great fun!
Dinner at almost midnight in Hemingway's bar on the Plaza de
Castile.

10,791 STEPS TODAY

END OF THE JOURNEY (FOR BULLS)
SUNDAY, JUNE 5, 2016
PAMPLONA
DAY 5

Left: A historical photograph of the Festival of San Fermin with the running of the bulls ending in the bullring

Pamplona

A red door marks the end of the journey for the bulls that run through the streets of Pamplona during the Festival of San Fermin. Behind the red door is Pamplona's bullring, and by the end of the afternoon the six bulls that thundered through the streets in the early morning, bowling over the runners who dared to challenge them, will themselves all be dead.

Next to the bullring there is a bust of Hemingway. Supposedly at the end of his life Hemingway regretted having made Pamplona, San Fermin, and the Running of the Bulls famous, since it allegedly ruined everything by attracting too many tourists. In Pamplona, however, the townspeople love Hemingway and what he has done for their city. Hemingway's image is everywhere.

After our late Saturday night out, first at Pablo Carbonell's show and then at our midnight visit with Hemingway at his bar, we slept in and had an easy Sunday. In the afternoon we took a walking tour around Pamplona as recommended by Rick Steves in his guidebook. (See Chapter 28, "Reading and Resources Suggestions," on page 242.)

7,825 STEPS TODAY

SPANNING TIME
MONDAY, JUNE 6, 2016
PAMPLONA TO PUENTE LA REINA
DAY 6

Pamplona

Puente La Reina

Puente La Reina (The Queens's Bridge) has graced this hamlet since the 12th century. The guidebooks say that historians are not sure which of two queens had it built. What? If a king had built it, there would be no doubts about which king. But let me not get off on that particular hobbyhorse. How many millions of pilgrims' feet have traversed these stones? What a timeless, serene, and beautiful image it is for this town.

On this day, James and I started our new regime of going by bus halfway and walking the rest of the way, about 10 kilometers. Better and easier for us! More time for reading and napping and having a leisurely lunch. I think we may have finally hit our stride.

23,510 STEPS TODAY

This very beautiful bridge has been in use for hundreds of years, allowing countless pilgrims to pass from one bank of the Arga River to the other.

Vineyards and Olive Orchards
Tuesday, June 7, 2016
Puente La Reina to Estella
Day 7

Estella •   ♾• Puente La Reina

Walking from Cirauqui to Lorca we saw our first (of many) sizeable vineyards and olive orchards. The ground is dry and rocky. The sun is very hot. The sky is very blue.

Implementing our new walking policy, we planned to take the bus to Lorca and then walk into Estella from there. When we stepped onto the bus, however, we were told that our only two choices were to get off at Cirauqui or to ride all the way to Estella. Having to make an instant decision and wanting to walk at least part of the way, we elected to get off at Cirauqui.

In Cirauqui we found the Camino and started off. It was an unexpectedly really hot day. For a good part of the time, we walked along a Roman road—rounded, uneven stones. I was thrilled to be on this historic road, but the footing was treacherous, so I was inching along.

And then my bad shoulder started aching again, so I gave my water to James. When we staggered into Lorca, we dropped at the first bar and guzzled liquids. The kindly bar keeper gave us an excellent gazpacho (cold) soup for lunch and then phoned a taxi for us. And off to Estella we went. Our new travel policy still needs fine tuning!

13,912 STEPS TODAY

*This part of the Camino wends its way through orchards
and wheat fields.*

This fountain is famous along the Camino. Free wine is dispensed.
The grey sign bears a poem: "Usage guidelines: We invite you with
pleasure, To Drink a Limited Measure. In order to take wine away,
We ask you to pay." The monks in this monastery are very up to date.
The red sign on the left advises visitors a webcam is watching.

This very beautiful cloister is perfumed by tall roses.

MONASTERIES AND CHURCHES, IRON AND ROSES
WEDNESDAY, JUNE 8, 2016
ESTELLA TO LOS ARCOS
DAY 8

Estella

Los Arcos •

Church of
Santa Maria

Our day started with a stop at a monastery and went on to include
a memorable church.

Our first stop after leaving Estella, just out of town, was the
Irache Monastery, where Benedictine monks make wine. The monks
have a wall-mounted fountain offering free wine and water. Their
sign invites visitors to enjoy a cup of wine on them, but asks for
those who want more wine please to purchase a bottle. The flaw in
this arrangement was that the monastery wine shop had not yet
opened when we stopped. James partook of the wine, but it was too
early for me.

We walked past an iron worker's workshop. I stopped to admire
some of his pieces, and he invited us in to see others. Wonderful work,
but very, very heavy. I thought about buying a piece, a beautiful wine
bottle stand, but decided to think about it and perhaps buy it online
and have it shipped.

We saw roses everywhere throughout the day, some with huge
blooms.

Late in the afternoon we visited the Church of Santa Maria,
which had a fabulously beautiful cloister, in the center of which was
a rather overgrown, unkempt bed of roses. There is symbolism
there—the religious fervor of those earlier Christians who built the
church versus the inattentiveness of the current era.

Tweaking our updated travel plan, we took off walking early in the day. Spain seems to be having an unexpectedly early heat wave, and we need to take advantage of the coolness in the early mornings. This turned out well. We had time in the late afternoon to visit the church and admire its beautiful cloister.

18,777 STEPS TODAY

THE STRAIGHT AND NARROW
THURSDAY, JUNE 9, 2016
LOS ARCOS TO VIANA
DAY 9

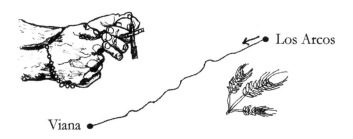

We left Los Arcos fairly early. The road had a good surface, through vineyards and wheat fields glowing golden in the sun. I met four pilgrims from Louisiana, and we chatted at Sansol after hop-scotching each other as we walked along. Just up the road from Sansol we caught the bus at Torres del Rio to take us into Viana.

The Camino surface was generally hard and firm, good footing. There was little shade, though, so when we made it to Sansol we sat down for drinks at the first café we came to. Then a long lunch at Torres del Rio while waiting for the bus. I used the time to upload photos. I'm still struggling with the technology!

18,300 STEPS TODAY

PILGRIMS' PROGRESS
FRIDAY, JUNE 10, 2016
VIANA TO LOGROÑO
DAY 10

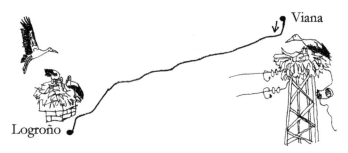

Leaving Viana, we saw a beautiful portal and stepped through, expecting to see a historic church. Instead, all was ruin, the evidence of time.

Coming into Logroño, we saw storks flying overhead, and then their nests on top of poles and spires. We crossed the bridge over the Ebro River and made our way to the Pilgrims' Fountain (pictured above), which has above it the escutcheon for Logroño.

A medieval fair is in town, and we briefly stopped at some booths along the route to our hotel. Later, waiting for my laundry, I sat near an elderly gentleman who clearly delighted in feeding the doves. He didn't mind having his picture taken either!

We pilgrims are suffering from the walking and the constant moving from day to day. I caught a cold in Pamplona, which has now jumped over to James. Lots of aches and pains.

28,432 STEPS TODAY

FAIR LOGROÑO
SATURDAY, JUNE 11, 2016
LOGROÑO
DAY 11

Logroño

Cheese vendor

Medieval musicians

The Saint Bernabe Fair was in full swing in Logroño. Buskers and fairgoers dressed in medieval and regional costumes were out in full force. Stalls were everywhere, with huge cheese wheels and delicious regional sweets on sale. The streets were thronged with families out until midnight. Rick Steves in his book on Spain says Logroño is skippable, but we found the fair to be great fun.

We also visited St. James Church, where Josemaría Escrivá, the founder of Opus Dei, worshipped and discovered his vocation. Michener has a lot to say in *Iberia* about Opus Dei and its influence in Spain and elsewhere.

We took photos of costumed street performers, some playing bagpipes. Evidently bagpipes are a traditional instrument of this region.

This was a rest day, and we needed it. James is feeling really poorly with his cold.

6,760 STEPS TODAY

NÁJERA CLOSES ITS DOORS
SUNDAY, JUNE 12, 2016
LOGROÑO TO NÁJERA
DAY 12

Logroño

Nájera

In contrast to Logroño, which had been so lively with the fair, Nájera felt dead. Closed up. We went to see the Monastery, Santa Maria la Real, which has the tombs of a number of very early kings and queens. It was closed. I asked a gentleman standing outside a side chapel door if it would open later in the afternoon. "No," he said. "It's Sunday."

"How about Monday morning?" I asked, thinking to stop in before we headed off.

"No," he replied. "It's closed on Mondays." No monastery for us.

On the way back to the hotel, I spied a shop with lovely Spanish ceramics (ceramics are a weakness of mine) in the window and an open shop door. I went in. A lady immediately came over and began shooing me out.

"A quick look around, please," I implored.

"No," she replied, "it's Sunday. We're closed."

On down the street, we did see a church open for business—a funeral. The street outside the church was packed with people; obviously the whole town had turned out. I was surprised, since at home funerals usually aren't held on Sundays.

Anyway, we can't tell you much about Nájera, since it turned its back to us, except that there were a lot of interesting shields and escutcheons on the outsides of buildings.

This day presented a lot of problems for us. Two issues combined to stop us from walking. First, James was feeling really poorly. Second, we couldn't discover an intermediate bus stop between Logroño and Nájera, so we took the bus the whole way. Then I made a mistake and started using my camera rather than my phone or tablet to take photos. This has turned out to be a big technological interface problem that I have spent hours and hours on, but can't solve.

9,986 STEPS TODAY

I've been to a lot of churches over the years, but I've never seen chickens living in a church before as honored residents, pampered and protected behind a beautiful grill.

This golden statue of Santo Domingo is just one of many in this town.

CHICKENS IN THE CHURCH
MONDAY, JUNE 13, 2016
NÁJERA TO SANTO DOMINGO DE LA CALZADA
DAY 13

Santo
Domingo de
la Calzada

Nájera

What a change from Nájera to Santo Domingo de la Calzada!

The cathedral was open for business, and full of visitors there to see the famous cock and hen, kept in a lovely coop high up on the cathedral wall. These are the only chickens in a church in Christendom, allowed to be there by a specific papal ruling. The chickens are supposed to be the direct descendants of the original miraculous chickens. In the tale, a cooked cock and hen sprang back to life, fully fledged, in order to prove the innocence of a falsely accused pilgrim.

Santo Domingo himself, who is buried in the cathedral, is a delightful saint. Turned away by two snobby monasteries who thought he was too stupid to be a monk, he dedicated his life to helping pilgrims and ended up with a town and cathedral named after him.

Although James was still not feeling well, we did walk halfway to Santo Domingo. While James slept in the afternoon, I explored the cathedral and a souvenir shop or two. In the evening James and I returned to the cathedral for a guided tour.

The guide was a very erudite gentleman who seemed to take delight in debunking some Christian myths. He pointed out what I already knew—from living in Portugal—that the story of chickens springing back to life is a common tale from many places in Europe. Santo Domingo de la Calzada has the distinction, though, of backing up the story by keeping chickens in the cathedral and by having had a pope give his backing to the miracle.

18,112 STEPS TODAY

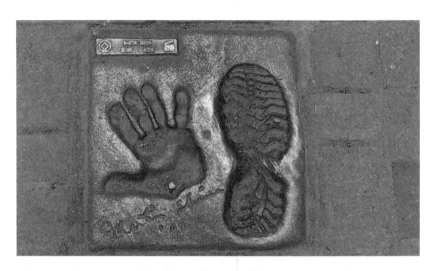

Here are Martin Sheen's handprint, footprint, and signature on a plaque set into the sidewalk. This plaque is one of many about the cast and crew of a film about the Camino, The Way.

Belorado abounds in lovely murals and mosaics.

THE CAMINO MEETS *THE WAY*
TUESDAY, JUNE 14, 2016
SANTO DOMINGO DE LA CALZADA TO BELORADO
DAY 14

Belorado

Santo
Domingo de
la Calzada

We walked from Santo Domingo to Redecilla del Camino, then
took a bus the rest of the way. It was another great day for walking—
cool, overcast, and good road surfaces.

On entering Belorado, one of the first things we stumbled upon
was this plaque, set into the pavement stones, showing actor Martin
Sheen's footprint, handprint, and signature. As we walked through
the town, which obviously has gone to a great effort to beautify the
streets, we saw many more of these plaques for other actors associated
with the film *The Way.*

It was fun to seek out Emilio Estevez's plaque and to try to figure
out to whom the other plaques pertained. I was told that in the tourist
information office they give out maps showing where all the plaques
are. It is Belorado's own version of the famous Hollywood Walk of
Fame. Obviously, the cast of *The Way* beat us to Belorado. Nobody
asked us for our handprint or footprint. (Regrettably waiters did ask
me for my signature on charge slips.)

We ducked into the local church for a quick look. The priest was
leading choir members and pilgrims in an international religious
sing-along. Then we went to a local restaurant where we were invited
to join five other pilgrims for a convivial dinner. Great fun!

23,137 STEPS TODAY

WHO IS THAT MASKED MAN?
WEDNESDAY, JUNE 15, 2016
BELORADO TO BURGOS
DAY 15

The road between Belorado and Espinosa del Camino was good. Over the past few days, we had been extraordinarily blessed with good weather—cool, overcast, and windy. So very windy, in fact, that James employed a bandana to keep the grit out of his still-congested mouth and noise.

This day showed one of the glitches of our walk-ride half-fast plan. We walked halfway, but then there was no bus to our next end-of-*stage* stopping point, San Juan de Ortega. We elected to take the bus all the way to Burgos, where we were spending the night anyway.

At lunchtime, before we caught the bus, a small Camino drama occurred. Two girls came into the restaurant where we were eating, one of them crying. They tried to explain to the restaurant head in English what had happened, but they couldn't surmount the language barrier.

I was called in to translate, which I did. The girls had been ripped off by an unscrupulous albergue (hostel) manager, who also threatened to sic the police on them. The restaurant owner was able to assure them not to worry, though he was unable to help them recover the money the guy had taken from them.

Once we were on the bus, the rain started pelting down, and we felt lucky to be out of it. By the time we reached Burgos, cool had turned to cold, the start of an unseasonable cold snap. In Burgos, our first city since Pamplona, we did some shopping for items we needed—Velcro, skin lotion, a cable to connect my camera to my tablet. This was my second (unsuccessful) attempt to solve this technology black hole.

21,976 STEPS TODAY

I don't want to say that I am obsessed with ceilings, but I do like to check them out. There are some amazing ceilings along the Camino. This one in Burgos Cathedral is stunning, but it is just one of the many beautiful ceilings in the cathedral.

Burgos Cathedral is a marvel, both inside and out. This amazing doorway is a sight to behold!

BURGOS CATHEDRAL
THURSDAY, JUNE 16, 2016
BURGOS
DAY 16

Burgos

After breakfast, we headed out for a guitar store. (James has been bemoaning his inability to practice during this extended trip.) What better place to purchase a guitar than Spain? This guitar can be James's major memento of the Camino.

On the way, we saw an open church and popped in. Saint Lesmes, whose lovely mausoleum is right there in the center of the church, is the patron saint of Burgos.

At the guitar shop James tried out many guitars, then selected a full-size Alhambra. He returned to the hotel while I went searching for an Internet café or something similar, still trying to solve my camera problem.

In the afternoon we were off to the Cathedral for an extended visit. Burgos Cathedral is the third largest in Spain, with only the cathedrals in Seville and Toledo being larger. Besides the central nave and aisles, there are many, many side chapels (eighteen, I think).

As one guidebook said, any one of these chapels, transferred to a museum in the USA, would be considered a masterwork of the collection. Here, all crowded together, it becomes, as James remarked, "overwhelming." So much beauty crowded into such a relatively small area!

The Cathedral also boasts a two-story cloister, something I have never seen before. I was particularly impressed with the cupolas and ceilings. Like the one pictured here, several of them are spectacular.

Burgos is also crowded with mementos of El Cid, an interesting hero since he fought for both Christian kings and Muslim overlords. El Cid is buried in the cathedral, and we took a photo of his gravestone.

We had hoped to go to a musical performance in the evening, but we were just too tired.

13,179 STEPS TODAY

BURGOS, CONTINUED
FRIDAY, JUNE 17, 2016
BURGOS
DAY 17

Burgos

Burgos was cold and rainy for our entire visit. Professor Henry Higgins may teach Eliza Doolittle that the rain in Spain falls mainly on the plain, but our experience is that it all lands on Burgos.

The town's squares are anything but square, all being eccentrically shaped. We walked through many of them multiple times—El Cid Plaza, Freedom Plaza, Plaza Mayor, etc.—but none of them looked like a traditional, central city, Spanish plaza. Burgos certainly has its own character!

Today was errands day. We spent the morning tracking down a laundromat. This was not an easy task to accomplish. Burgos doesn't seem to have many laundromats, despite being a city. We had to walk a long way, our dirty clothes in our backpacks, to find the closest one.

In the afternoon, we went back to the music store, where James exchanged his full-sized guitar for a smaller, traveling one that will fit in his backpack. Then he went back to the hotel before his new guitar got rained on, while I carried on trying, unsuccessfully, to solve my camera problems by visiting a camera store and then a phone store. After wasting multiple hours over several days trying to fix this issue, I finally gave up.

With James bummed out about having to give up his full-sized guitar and me grumpy about not being able to use my camera, we went out to dinner to change the mood via ordering roast pig—a specialty at the restaurant we went to and an homage to Michener, who recounted in *Iberia* searching all over Spain for the best roast pig. Along with our *cochino asado* (roast pig), we downed a pitcher of sangria. Not a bad way to end the day.

13,547 STEPS TODAY

Note the abandoned hiking boots, hanging from the tree like Camino decorations.

HANGING SHOES
SATURDAY, JUNE 18, 2016
BURGOS TO HORNILLOS AND ISAR
DAY 18

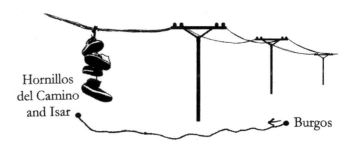

Hornillos
del Camino
and Isar

Burgos

Leaving Burgos, we walked along the street on the high side of the cathedral. From that perspective, the cathedral's spires were gorgeously outlined against the blue sky. Our departure took us by the University of Burgos, which looked to be a thoroughly modern campus. Once out in the countryside, we saw how rocky yet fertile the soil is. And with less to look at, we had time to observe some things more closely.

All along the Way we have seen discarded objects. Mostly they have been hiking boots and athletic shoes, but once we even saw an abandoned metal suitcase out in the middle of nowhere. At first, the discarded items were usually left on roadside markers or on piles of stones, but folks are getting more creative.

We saw a couple of variations of hanging shoes on this day. The first one was as we walked through the university, and I suspect students might have been responsible for that one. But the tableau in the photo is quite far out in the countryside. I couldn't help thinking of the Clint Eastwood film, *Hang 'Em High*. I think a number of those so-called spaghetti westerns of his were actually shot here in Spain rather than in Italy.

We had planned to walk to Tardajos and take a bus from there. The hotel receptionist in Burgos had told us, after phoning the bus station, that there was a Tardajos-Hornillos bus. It tuned out that the information was wrong. No buses served Tardajos.

We asked about taxis, but they wanted 30€ for ten kilometers, so we walked the whole way. This was one the few times we did the whole distance, twenty-one kilometers, double our usual amount. Camino conditions were good—a cool day, a relatively flat road, and a good road surface except for the last steep decline into Hornillos, when I used my walking sticks. We actually stayed in a nice *casa rural* in Isar, an even smaller village not far from Hornillos.

37,430 STEPS TODAY

ANGEL OF MERCY
SUNDAY, JUNE 19, 2016
ISAR TO CASTROJERIZ
DAY 19

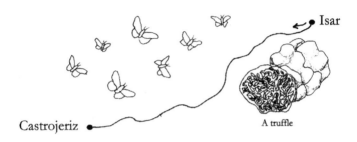

A truffle

These small towns on the Meseta are almost ghost towns, with tiny populations. Without the influx of business from pilgrims, some of them probably would be ghost towns. This was the day of the white butterflies and of Angel The Truffle Hunter. The butterflies fluttered all around us, and sometimes I shortened my step to avoid running into one. I've seen them elsewhere, but not in such numbers as here.

We walked from Hornillos to Hontanas. A nice, cool day, but a very rocky road. My left pinkie toe was really complaining. In Hontanas, we had lunch, and then I asked the barkeep to phone for a taxi for me. A guy sitting at the bar offered to drive me. (See Chapter 13, "The Truffle Hunter," on page 61.) I wish I had taken a photo of Angel, but I didn't.

20,750 STEPS TODAY

ROMANESQUE THE BEST, SAYS MICHENER
MONDAY, JUNE 20, 2016
CASTROJERIZ TO FROMISTA
DAY 20

St. Martin Church

←● Castrojeriz

Fromista ●

When we arrived in Fromista, the church door was open, so we immediately went in. St. Martin Church was a charming, pure Romanesque church. James Michener wrote about his high regard for Romanesque and how he preferred it to Gothic. I wondered if this was the church he wrote about, but it wasn't. He would have loved it.

Facing a twenty-four kilometer *stage*, with James's foot hurting and no bus service to an intermediate town, we elected to take a taxi to Fromista. I ended up being very pleased with this decision since it allowed us to tour St. Martin's, across the plaza from our hotel. We had a lovely, though too expensive, a la carte lunch on the terrace facing the church.

Lots of problems with the Internet. It is just not robust enough in these small towns to support uploading photographs, and I get tired of fighting the technology.

4,508 STEPS TODAY

YOU CAN'T MAKE THIS STUFF UP: TEEPEES, GEESE, DONKEYS, AND
  THE ALMOND MAN
TUESDAY JUNE 21, 2016
FROMISTA TO CARRION DE LOS CONDES
DAY 21

Carrion de
los Condes

Fromista

This was a day with many unusual sights. We saw teepees, but
never got an explanation as to why they were there. (They're shown
in one of my map books, so they have been there for a while.) We
stopped to rehydrate at one albergue and found ourselves in a magical
menagerie garden with geese, chickens, and even donkeys joining the
pilgrims for a snack.

Walking down a long, straight stretch, we saw ahead a car
parked beside the road. As we got closer, we saw that a gentleman of
advanced years was dispensing something to passing pilgrims. It was
almonds. If he had time between pilgrims, he would crack them for
you. Otherwise, a handful of unshelled nuts for your pocket.

The girl ahead of me got a kiss on the cheek. I got the kiss, both
cracked and uncracked nuts, a mini-muffin, and a chocolate. James
got uncracked nuts. Along the Camino you sometimes find spontaneous generosity and kindness like this. (See Chapter 12, "The
Almond Man," on page 57.)

This was another day with no intermediate bus stop. We started
out walking, thinking maybe we would catch a taxi when we got too
tired. In the end, we walked the full way, with two stops for drinks
and a longish lunch break, during which we chatted with two

Americans. It was a very hot day, but the road surface was great. All in all, an interesting day despite the sameness of the countryside.

31,978 STEPS TODAY

FAITH AND FARMING
WEDNESDAY, JUNE 22, 2016
CARRION DE LOS CONDES TO TERRADILLOS
   TO CALZADILLA DE LA CUEZA
DAY 22

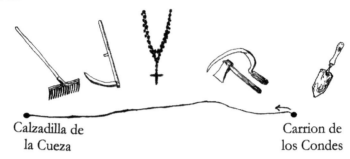

Calzadilla de
la Cueza

Carrion de
los Condes

After our long walk the previous day, we definitely wanted an easier day. Again, there was no bus to where we wanted to go, but there was a bus to a town farther along the Camino, Terradillos, so we took that. Although I don't like backtracking, that is what we had to do. The bus didn't leave until noon, so I used the morning for errands and to explore Carrion a bit.

I had to go to three ATMs, then eventually return back to the first one before I could extract any funds. It was like a comedy of errors—ATM style. Nothing seemed to work in Carrion. I couldn't buy our bus tickets on the first try either. While waiting to buy the tickets, I popped into a couple of small shops and then took some photos. Eventually I was able to buy the bus tickets. All the while James rested up; his feet have been bothering him.

Once we got to the town to which the bus went, Terradillos, we had to find a taxi to take us back to Calzadilla, where we had reservations for the night. We went in an *albergue* (hostel) for a drink and to order a taxi. I thought the decorations on the wall in the *albergue* fairly well summed up what we had been seeing on the Meseta: agriculture combined with great religious faith.

6,141 STEPS TODAY

Along the Camino, there is a lot of public art, much of it showing St. James or pilgrims or Saint James as a pilgrim. Here, the traditional pilgrim's gourd has been replaced by a copper water bottle.

WASTED DAYS AND WASTED NIGHTS
THURSDAY, JUNE 23, 2016
CALZADILLA DE LA CUEZA TO PUERTA DE SAHAGUN
DAY 23

Puerta de
Sahagun

Calzadilla de
la Cueza

Relative to the very small towns in which we had been staying, Sahagun was decent sized. Lots of public art, such as this pilgrim in metal.

We had booked a taxi to take us from Calzadilla to Sahagun, but the driver didn't show up at the agreed hour, so the hotel owner drove us there.

Once in Sahagun, we were both tired, so we had long siestas and then dinner. James ordered spaghetti, but when it came it had egg in it, so he wouldn't eat it. Amazingly, spaghetti—the so-typical dish of Italy—is almost always among the choices on the pilgrim's menu for the first course. I guess it is there because it is inexpensive to make and filling, but perhaps also because it is a popular choice.

James orders it fairly frequently. He always asks what is in it first, but this time the waiter didn't say that it came with visible boiled egg bits in it. The waiter graciously swapped out the spaghetti for a different dish.

These two acts of kindness by hotel staff along the way—one by the hotel owner offering to drive us himself to our next stop and then the waiter swapping dishes—are representative of the very nice staff we have met all along our journey.

I took almost no steps today, and my feet were happy. Even so, I couldn't help but hear, on a repeated loop running through my head, the Freddy Fender classic song about wasted days and nights.

2,657 STEPS TODAY

LAUNDRY DAY
FRIDAY, JUNE 24, 2016
PUERTA DE SAHAGUN
DAY 24

Puerta de Sahagun

Right next to our hotel stood a very old building. I didn't see a plaque or any indication of why it had been allowed to continue standing. It was a very visible reminder of old building styles in Spain, and looked quite different from all of the brick and stucco buildings around it.

When setting up my schedule, I built a rest day into it every week. Besides rest, I planned to use the day for laundry and other necessary tasks. Sahagun, though a somewhat larger town, foiled me. There was no laundromat in the town.

The hotel receptionist suggested that I try using the machines in the *albergue* across the street. (While our hotel did not have laundry facilities, the hostel across the street did have a washer and dryer.) That suggestion sounded like a good idea to me. I could go over and wash clothes early, before the next batch of pilgrims arrived in town.

As a result, at 10:00 am, I was sitting on the steps of the *albergue* with my laundry, reading and waiting for the *albergue* to open. (Opening time was announced as 10:00 am on a large sign posted right by the front door.) 10:00 am came and went. Then 10:30 am. Then 11:00 am.

By this time, I was getting nervous. We could have the hotel wash our clothes, but it would be much more expensive and we had to turn the clothes in by noon. At 11:45 am, I gave up on the *albergue* and went in and turned our clothes over to the hotel, which promised to have them done "by nine."

The *albergue* finally opened its door at around 12:15 pm, while James and I were sitting on the terrace in front of our hotel having a drink. No one I asked seemed to know the reason for the delay in opening. We saw lots of early arriving pilgrims from 10:00 am to noon shake their heads in bewilderment and then move on when they got no response to pounding on the door. At least we just had laundry troubles, not housing concerns! Another lazy day for us.

4,017 STEPS TODAY

The Camino in general is very safe in terms of there being little crime, but the journey is arduous. Memorial crosses along the Way are not uncommon, though this is a particularly beautiful one.

PEREGRINOS WHO HAVE PASSED
SATURDAY, JUNE 25, 2016
PUERTA DE SAHAGUN TO EL BURGO RANERO
DAY 25

It turned out that our laundry wasn't ready the previous night at 9:00 pm, as I thought had been promised, or even at 9:00 am the following morning. After we finally got the laundry back, we sorted and packed it as quickly as possible, but even so, for the first time during the trip, we had the luggage delivery guy pounding on our door asking about our luggage.

Back on the road again, we had good walking conditions. A cool day, and a good road surface. Along the way, we met Veronica from Romania at a crossroads where we were puzzling out which of three possible roads to follow. We ran into her again at a café at lunchtime. Veronica told us that she is a journalist back in Romania and is filing a report every day about her Camino.

James is tired of always seeing the same options on the menu. Our "mixed salad" at lunch consisted of tuna, green olives, and tomatoes—no lettuce whatsoever.

On the Camino, there are plentiful reminders of pilgrims who have gone before us—and frequent reminders of our mortality. I haven't seen any statistics on how many pilgrims die while walking the Camino, but given how much it taxes everyone, even the physically fit, I am not surprised to come across memorial crosses like the one in the photo. Of course, the movie *The Way* starts with a father trying to understand how his son perished on the Camino and why the son so wanted to make this journey. R.I.P., Mr. Friedrich, and all the other *peregrinos* who have passed while on the Camino.

30,452 STEPS TODAY

TERRORISTS EVERYWHERE
SUNDAY, JUNE 26, 2016
EL BURGO RANERO TO MANSILLA DE LAS MULAS
DAY 26

When I passed this sign for a flying school out in the middle of nowhere, I couldn't help but think about terrorism, the scourge of our time. It was an eerie foreshadowing of the next day's news about the Istanbul airport bombing. Before I delayed my trip by a month, I had been scheduled to transit that airport around this date on my return trip home.

Having learned about the paucity of buses in general on the Meseta and the specific lack of buses on weekends, I did not even investigate the bus situation. We set out walking on what turned out to be another cool day with a good road surface. James lagged behind me, and when I stopped for lunch at Reliegos, it took him quite a while to catch up. I hadn't realized how far behind he was. When he arrived, he said that his foot was hurting.

We met up with Veronica from Romania again, and had lunch with her and Randy from Miami. Veronica, it turns out, is walking the Camino to raise funds for a charity. She explained that volunteerism and giving to charities is not well developed in Romania due to its communist background, so that is a field she is working to advance.

And Randy is a Foreign Service brat, so he and James had that in common. An interesting lunch, then six more kilometers to our designated stopping place for the night.

31,031 STEPS TODAY

STAINED GLASS SOARING TO HEAVEN
MONDAY, JUNE 27, 2016
MANSILLA DE LAS MULAS TO LEÓN
DAY 27

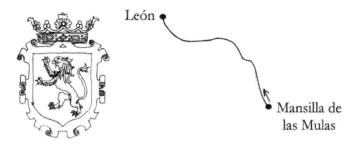

After two days of long walks, we took the bus to León. The symbol of the former Kingdom of León (currently the Spanish province of León) is of course the lion, and no doubt many assume that León has always been the name of this place. In fact, the name was derived from the Latin word for "legion," and indeed one of the Roman legions was based here.

Our hotel is part of St. Isidoro Monastery. We are so lucky to be staying in this historic and gorgeous place. Right after checking in, we and other hotel guests were treated to a tour of the monastery by the hotel manager.

After lunch, we headed over to see the cathedral and its museum. The cathedral is so beautiful, with more stained glass than any other cathedral in Europe except for Chartres in France. Our photos cannot capture the beauty of that glass, since the brilliant light tends to bleed the color to just white. (The stained-glass image on the cover of this book is from León Cathedral.)

James Michener writes about this glowing cathedral glass in *Iberia*. Indeed, the architects of the cathedral stretched the amount of wall given over to glass to the maximum, making an already unstable building (due to being built over Roman baths and other preexisting structures) even more unstable. A cupola collapsed at one point, and there was real fear that the whole cathedral would tumble down before extensive renovations were carried out.

It is amazing to learn that this cathedral was built in just fifty years by a town with a population of only 5,000. Its purity of line was no doubt helped by that rapid building spree. The León Cathedral was built to compete with the Burgos Cathedral, and indeed it does. Both are magnificent, but they are very, very different.

After leaving the cathedral, we had sangria on the plaza in front. Spain had a soccer game scheduled for that evening in the European Cup competition, and young people draped in Spanish flags were all over the plaza while loud rock music blared out from a party bus. It was really a happening scene, though to walk out from the serenity of the cathedral to rock & roll was a bit jarring.

I posted a photo of us on the APOC webpage, and we received lots of positive feedback from that.

Then back to the hotel, where James rested while I went to the pilgrim's mass at 7:00 pm. The quick mass was followed by a special blessing for the pilgrims in attendance. I was asked to translate Father Pascual's words of welcome and blessing into English, which I did. It was a very beautiful blessing.

I gathered up James and we went to an Italian restaurant for something different from the usual choices on the pilgrim's menu. As it happens, León is in the middle of celebrating a week of festivities in honor of St. Peter and St. Paul, with many cultural activities around town. Finished with dinner, we headed for an outdoor pop concert being given as part of the festival. We stayed until the end, then walked back to the hotel at midnight. James enjoyed the music.

I took many, many photos of León, James's favorite city so far.

13,188 STEPS TODAY

THE CHALICE
TUESDAY, JUNE 28, 2016
LEÓN
DAY 28

León

We had breakfast but then lazed around the hotel since James's foot continues to hurt. At noon we went to the St. Isidoro Museum and Pantheon and lucked into a guided tour in Spanish. St. Isidoro in León is an amazing place. The church is lovely and houses the bones of this early Spanish saint. The pantheon has tombs of princes and nobility.

The museum is the home of the Holy Grail. Photos weren't permitted in the museum, so I don't have an original photo of the Grail. The one above is a photo from the book I am currently reading (yes, yet another book) about the Grail. The book recounts research undertaken at the Al Azhar University archives in Cairo that strengthens the provenance of St. Isidoro's chalice.

While there are contending chalices in some other countries, none is as well documented as this one, according to the authors. It is truly a beautiful piece, and it gives one goosebumps to think of being so close to such a sacred object.

After lunch at a nearby restaurant, James rested while I went to a washateria and caught up on laundry. That evening, there was a concert in the cloister of St. Isidoro. We went early and managed to snag chairs.

The most memorable piece, at least for me, was a reading of segments out of Don Quijote, accompanied by music specifically composed for those segments. As the beautifully voiced gentleman read the story of the knight of La Mancha and his trusty sidekick Sancho Panza, thanks to the musicians we heard the wind rustling through the fields and the clip-clop of the hooves of Don Quijote and Sancho's steeds. It was a standing-room only audience.

After the concert, we had a late dinner in St. Isidoro Plaza, where a lot of the musicians dropped by for a post-concert drink and tapas. This was the last night of León's festival, and clearly music lovers from all over the city turned out for this concluding concert.

10,962 STEPS TODAY

GUESS WHO IS COMING TO BREAKFAST?
WEDNESDAY, JUNE 29, 2016
LEÓN TO VILLAR DE MAZARIFE (VILLAVANTE)
DAY 29

León

Villavante   Villar de Mazarife

On our last morning in León, who should appear in the hotel's breakfast room but Father Pascual, the priest who gave the pilgrims' blessing the night before. We chatted for a bit. He is one of eight priests at St. Isidoro's. That sounds like a lot, but a number of them go out and serve at rural parishes that have no resident priest. He allowed me to take his photograph.

While James rested, I took a last walk around the city to see a few places I hadn't had a chance to see. I saw an ancient plaza whose cobblestones appear to be just the way they were hundreds of years ago. Then with James, we took a bus to Villar de Mazarife, where we had lunch, and which was our scheduled stopping point for the day.

Our lodging for the night was actually farther down the road, in Villavante. The owner of the place picked us up and drove us to his compound, a charming *casa rural* (a house in the countryside that is licensed by the government of Spain to offer accommodations).

We had dinner there with other guests: a Spanish couple from Mallorca, a Mexican-American couple from California, and three other Americans. It was a very convivial evening, conducted in Spanish and English, with lots of jokes and stories.

The Mexican-American pilgrim is a dedicated marathoner, but he said that the Camino is taxing even his endurance, and his wife had outpaced him that day.

James's foot is still hurting, and I told him that I think it is time to seek out a doctor, even though he doesn't want to. When we lunched with Veronica and Randy back in Reliegos, they each said that they had already been to the hospital more than once. Obviously, pilgrims are giving doctors in northern Spain a lot of business, and in particular a lot of experience with foot problems!

13,998 STEPS TODAY

TOP LANCE
THURSDAY, JUNE 30, 2016
VILLAVANTE TO HOSPITAL DE ORBIGO
DAY 30

Hospital de Orbigo

Villavante

From Villavante, the walk into Hospital de Orbigo was only three kilometers or so. Once we checked into the hotel, we rested and then I read and worked on the blog. James's foot has not improved at all.

Hospital de Orbigo is the site of a famous historical feat of arms. In the Middle Ages, knights from all across Europe came to Spain to protect pilgrims from raids by Moors and attacks by brigands. One Spanish knight, Suero de Quiñones, became annoyed by other knights boasting that they were the bravest, or the strongest, or the best fighter along the Camino. He therefore challenged all comers to "put up or shut up" by meeting him in single combat, one by one, at the bridge in Hospital de Orbigo.

Come they did, and Suero began jousting against them. After a while, nine other Spanish knights joined him, and they too took on all challengers. Suero was an outstanding fighter, and he won all of his jousts. Chroniclers of the time reported that as many as 700 jousts occurred over a period of thirty days.

The Church finally stopped the jousting after one knight was accidentally killed (by his own lance when it broke). After that, at least during Suero's lifetime, there was no more boasting by other knights along Suero's stretch of the Camino.

From the balcony of our hotel, we overlooked the modern jousting field. Each year, thousands pour into Hospital de Orbigo on June 1st to see a series of jousts held on the field to commemorate Suero's feats of bravery. Suero was also madly in love with a lady, and wore an iron collar once a week to prove his love. What a knight!

I was torn about whether to post a photo of the jousting field or a good shot of the beautiful Roman bridge, but since I have already posted a picture of the Roman bridge at Puente La Reina and since the story of Suero de Quiñones is so unique, I went with the jousting field. The Roman bridge is located next to the jousting field.

At dinner, we chatted with a German couple from Frankfurt. I had met the gentleman previously, after the pilgrims' blessing in León, when he thanked me for doing the Spanish-English translation of the blessing.

8,649 STEPS TODAY

A NOT-SO-GAUDY GAUDI
FRIDAY, JULY 1, 2016
HOSPITAL DE ORBIGO TO ASTORGA
DAY 31

Astorga •   ↙ • Hospital
                                                                de Orbigo

We had a lovely breakfast on the terrace overlooking the Hospital de Orbigo jousting field. Then, off to catch the bus to Astorga.

After checking into our wonderful hotel right on the Plaza Mayor in Astorga, we booked a taxi to go to the emergency room to have James's foot looked at by a doctor. It's official: he has plantar fasciitis. The doctor prescribed strong ibuprofen, a cream for foot massages, and above all rest for his foot. With the doctor's orders ringing in our ears, I deposited James back at the hotel and then went to visit Gaudi's palace and the cathedral.

When I lived in Barcelona so many years ago, I regularly saw Catalan architect Antoni Gaudi's unfinished cathedral. I didn't care for it that much. Like Michener preferring Romanesque to Gothic, I sometimes prefer plain architecture rather than anything flamboyant, and in my opinion Gaudi's cathedral in Barcelona just takes things too far.

It was therefore a pleasure to see the restrained lines of his Archbishop's Palace in Astorga. The palace now serves as a museum, and is filled with wonderful artwork. Items from the Roman period are consigned to the basement, as perhaps is fitting for an archbishop's former place of residence. There is a room with every sort of Santiago statue that you can imagine: Santiago reading,

Santiago riding, Santiago praying, etc. I also visited the Astorga cathedral and its museum.

On the way back to the hotel, I bought chocolates for James and an Astorga pin for my cap. Dinner on the plaza in front of our hotel allowed us to watch the mechanical figures on the clock tower of the municipal building strike the quarter hours. What a treat, to balance the bad news about James's foot.

11,367 STEPS TODAY

This is the wrapper for a chocolate bar I purchased in Astorga. In the Chocolate Museum, there is a display about how chocolate has been marketed through the years, with chocolate items carrying images of everything from famous people to well-known local landmarks. I thought this wrapper to be particularly charming.

THE CHOCOLATE CAPITAL OF SPAIN
SATURDAY, JULY 2, 2016
ASTORGA TO RABANAL DEL CAMINO
DAY 32

After breakfast, we headed down to the Chocolate Museum. Walking through Astorga, every other shop is selling chocolate or ice cream or sweets. It turns out that Astorga is the chocolate capital of Spain. In the past, there were 400 artisanal chocolate-making workshops in Astorga. Once mass-production machines came on line, the number of these small workshops decreased, but there are still six of them in Astorga making chocolate the old-fashioned way.

Astorga has a Chocolate Museum, which both James and I visited. It made me think. Chocolate originally came from Mexico, but I don't remember ever seeing anything like a chocolate museum in Mexico. Maybe there is one, but if so I have never come across it.

It was very interesting to learn how chocolate is made. The Astorga chocolate connection evidently goes back to Hernan Cortes, who offered a chocolate monopoly as part of his daughter's dowry when she married into a prominent Astorgan family.

We had lunch in a café in the town, where we again ran into Tom from Germany. (This is our second Tom from Germany, so now we call the other Tom "Tom from Frankfurt.") This Tom is traveling alone and has kept pace with us for several weeks, and we regularly run into him. It was this Tom who suggested yesterday that we visit the Chocolate Museum. Great suggestion, Tom. Thanks!

Following lunch, the hotel called a taxi for us to go to Rabanal del Camino. Our taxi driver was the same one who had driven us to the emergency room the day before. He was very knowledgeable about the region and told us about the Camino in this area as he drove along.

6,897 STEPS TODAY

My son and I at the base of the Iron Cross. The pole on which it is mounted is so tall that we couldn't get it in the picture frame. Along with other pilgrims, here we left the stones we had carried since the start of our pilgrimage.

THE IRON CROSS
SUNDAY, JULY 3, 2016
RABANAL DEL CAMINO TO ACEBO
DAY 33

El Acebo de
San Miguel

Rabanal
del Camino

Juan Manuel Garcia Cuesta, our trusty taxi driver for two trips already, phoned late last night to say that he had a fare going to Rabanal and could then drive us to Acebo if we wished to hire him. Absolutely we wished!

We asked Juan Manuel to stop along the way at the Iron Cross, one of the most famous spots on the Camino. This is where pilgrims traditionally deposit a rock they have carried with them along the Camino. It symbolizes laying down a concern or burden that has been weighing them down.

I picked up my rock right outside of Saint-Jean-Pied-de-Port; it was fan shaped and reminded me of the Camino cockleshell. James wanted a river rock and diligently searched through several stream beds until he found what he was looking for. Both of our rocks ended their journey on this day.

My rock carried two concerns. I was not sure that I could actually lay one of them down, but maybe St. James would give me a bit of help.

Juan Manuel took this photo of us, using my tablet. (Unfortunately, the photo does not show the cross on the top of the pole.) Juan Manuel told us that some years back the pole was actually cut down by a malicious (or nutty) individual. The government replaced it, this time with interior reinforcement to thwart any future attempt to cut down the cross.

I wondered out loud why pilgrims laid down their burdens here rather than right outside Santiago de Compostela. Juan Manuel noted that back in the Middle Ages the Camino journey could take six months or more, so being a couple of weeks from the end of the journey perhaps felt like the end to them. As I thought about it, it occurred to me that perhaps pilgrims, having prayed and worried over their issue, wanted to lay down that burden and turn instead to preparing their hearts for a joyful entry into Santiago. I was a bit sorry to set my rock down, having grown attached to this inanimate object that symbolized so much for me.

After checking in at the *albergue* complex in which we are staying, we walked into the village, where we had lunch in the backyard of a cafe. The cafe advertised the backyard as a "terrace," but really it was just a backyard, with a few tables with umbrellas set up.

Next to us was a clothes line with pilgrims' clothes flapping in the breeze as they dried. Boy, those clothes looked raggedy. Three children scrambled around playing on some small plastic backyard playground equipment—a miniature slide, a rocking horse, and an auto. This lunch didn't quite reach the bucolic level of the lunch we had with the donkeys, geese, and chickens, but it was close.

In contrast, the *albergue* complex we are staying in is quite swanky. It has a swimming pool—the first swimming pool we have seen in Spain. The place was mobbed, with two large lunchtime gatherings and many family groups, plus several bands of teenagers. Of course, it was Sunday, a traditional day in Spain for family outings and lunches.

Several of the pilgrims staying here, enchanted by the pool and the other comforts, have decided to stay over an extra day. I have to say that sitting on the terrace (a real terrace) looking out over the valley, with a cool breeze flowing in, was very enjoyable. Good WiFi, too, which is wonderful. No struggling to up or download.

5,372 STEPS TODAY

OUTSIDE THE CASTLE
MONDAY, JULY 4, 2016
ACEBO TO PONFERRADA
DAY 34

Ponferrada

Happy Birthday, USA!

4th of July

El Acebo de
San Miguel

The highlight of the day was having lunch at a café across the street from the Templars Castle in Ponferrada, which is the best-preserved castle of the Knights Templar in Europe. It was truly an amazing view.

At breakfast in Acebo, I stood up and wished all the Americans present a happy 4th of July. There were quite a few American pilgrims there, so a small cheer went up. I told James that I would like to celebrate the day somehow, maybe by a special dinner. Several of the Americans to whom we talked decided to celebrate by staying an extra day at the comfortable hotel complex, sunning by the pool and having Spanish-style *carne asada* (barbeque). Not for us, but it sounded nice.

I booked a taxi to take us to Ponferrada at 11:00 am. In the meantime, I planned to walk back a short way down the road to the small, nearby village and look around, but instead I settled down and took advantage of the good WiFi to catch up on the blog.

Once in Ponferrada and checked in, we walked around the corner and had lunch across the street from the Knights Templar castle. I had planned to do laundry in the afternoon, but instead napped and read. In the evening, we had a very small 4th of July celebration—we ordered a la carte instead of the pilgrims' menu. It made a nice change.

3,201 STEPS TODAY

*This castle was a base for the Knights Templar guarding the
Camino. It is still a very impressive structure.*

*Looking down from the castle, one can see the river below.
The steep climb up from the river would make this side of the
castle even more impregnable. Today the town bumps up against the
castle on every side.*

THE CASTLE
TUESDAY, JULY 5, 2016
PONFERRADA
DAY 35

Ponferrada

Since the castle was built over many years, there are old parts, and even older parts. For example, there is the "Old Keep" and the "New Keep." The whole castle area is quite large, and there are still areas not rebuilt or even excavated by archeologists.

In the centuries after the castle stopped being used, a lot of its stones were recycled into neighboring churches and homes. The narrative film in the castle explains how the castle began to be preserved and then restored in the 1920s and afterwards, after first appearing as an emblematic photo in advertising, such as on chocolate bars.

The castle grounds also include a gallery devoted to facsimiles of medieval books, everything from books from around 800 AD to the start of printing. Facsimile copies of Books of Hours belonging to famous people are there, such as one belonging to Isabella of Castile. And there is a tournament book, owned by Rene of Anjou, that shows how knights fought and what jousting tournaments really looked like.

A separate area is given over to books about and research on the Knights Templar. For me, a book and history lover, this was all fabulous.

We made a long visit to the castle. Workmen were disassembling fireworks stands, removing glasses and food and drink, and taking down flags. Evidently, we had just missed the annual city celebration of the Knights Templar, the "Night of the Knight," which occurred over the previous weekend. I am sorry we missed it. It would have been a great substitute for our normal 4th of July celebration, given the fireworks, parade, etc.

We stopped in a church we had seen from the castle, and visited a shop with souvenirs and medieval gear like swords and gauntlets. (I thought of my brother Douglas, who used to participate in medieval reenactments. He would have loved the shop.) Then, after lunch, we headed for the laundromat.

We finished off the day with dinner at a really nice Italian restaurant. The lasagna was fabulous, and we ordered a bottle of Chianti, the most expensive wine on the wine list, I think, at 14€. This was James's first taste of Chianti, and he wanted to take the bottle with him, but of course we can't haul that bottle around for the rest of our trip. And so to bed, after a long day.

13,999 STEPS TODAY

SOLO TRAVELER
WEDNESDAY, JULY 6, 2016
PONFERRADA TO VILLAFRANCA
DAY 36

Villafranca
del Bierzo

Ponferrada

Author's Note: From this point forward, the entries come from my travel journal rather than my blog. I was getting too frustrated with trying to post daily updates and upload photos when the WiFi wouldn't cooperate. I thought perhaps I would catch up on posts when I got to a town with good connectivity, but, in the end, I didn't want to spend the time.

Today I arranged to split up from James for the day. I wanted to walk, but he couldn't. I booked a taxi to take James to the bus station. From there, he could take a bus to Villafranca, while I walked the Camino.

The path was so-so, with lots of rocks and gravel and some hills, but overall not too bad. The morning was very hot, then after lunch it began threatening rain with lots of thunder and lightning. Sprinkles of rain began, sometimes quite heavy sprinkles. Before it started pouring, I thought it prudent to make the necessary adjustments. I pulled out my waterproof Ziplock pouch and stored my phone and tablet in it.

Then I put on my rain poncho. Since I was by myself, it didn't go so well. My poncho kept snagging on my backpack, and I couldn't tug it free. Nor could I figure out what the poncho was catching on. I took off my poncho several times and put it back on, trying to fluff it out over my backpack, but each time I had the same problem.

This was the first time I had had to get my rain gear out of my backpack, and of course it was the day James wasn't with me. He could have fixed the problem in ten seconds, but I spent several minutes in the drizzle before giving up. If my backpack and the things in it got wet, so be it. My phone and tablet were safe, and that's all that really mattered.

I started off again with a still-snagged poncho. Eventually the wind freed the poncho. Despite all the menacing signs, the light rain never developed into a pouring deluge, as I had feared. My backpack and I survived quite nicely.

Along the way I saw some interesting folk art and stopped to look at it. A husband and wife offered me beer or water. Yet more kindness offered by strangers.

I ducked into an open church I saw for a quick peek and finally staggered into Villafranca at 6:45 pm. I had left Ponferrada at 9:00 am, so that was about nine hours of walking to reach my destination.

I met James at the hotel. I quickly showered, then rushed down, famished, to dinner at 7:15 pm. Over dinner we talked with a Scottish couple who were bicycling the Camino with their seven-year-old son. He was managing quite well, they said, and keeping up with them. We spoke about Brexit, Harry Potter, my visit to Scotland way back when, and many other topics.

The WiFi is very poor here. I struggled with it for a while, then turned in by 10:00 pm. I didn't sleep well, and was awake by 3:00 am. As usual when I can't sleep, I read until I could nod off.

43,176 STEPS TODAY

A Reading Break
Thursday, July 7, 2016
Villafranca to Las Herrerias
Day 37

Las Herrerias

Villafranca
del Bierzo

Once again, we faced transportation difficulties: there is no bus from Villafranca to Las Herrerias. James would have to take a taxi. I went back and forth in my mind about whether to walk or go in the taxi with James. Wednesday had been a hard day of walking, and James had spent the day alone. I decided to give myself a break and go in the taxi.

We arrived in Las Herrerias far in advance of the time we would have if we had walked. This is still chocolate country, so James and I drank hot chocolate on the hotel patio, his with a dash of liquor, mine without.

I found a left-behind copy of a James Patterson book, *Sail*, and decided to take a break from reading about Spain and the Camino. The book, about a family summer sailing trip that goes terribly awry, has at its center a dysfunctional family. In a weird way, the book made me feel better. My extended family has issues, that is for sure, but we aren't trying to kill each other to get our hands on the family fortune. Maybe not being wealthy has some silver linings.

James and I set off for the village to find a café for lunch. (Our hotel is outside of town.) We started walking, only to realize that we would have to walk up and down a hill to get there, under the hot midday sun. We turned around and headed back to the hotel to try its food.

Even though Las Herrerias is inland, like most restaurants in Spain the hotel restaurant served various seafood dishes. James and I had frequently ordered fried *calamares* (squid), but for the first time I asked for *pulpo* (octopus). It was delicious. The Spanish know to cook those two dishes.

After lunch, a nap and more reading. The fictional family is really in deep kimchi. It was hard to put the book down, but at 9:15 pm hunger got the best of me and I went downstairs to eat. It's a good thing the Spanish keep late dining hours. James wasn't hungry, so he stayed upstairs.

After dinner, I sat in the hotel's lounge and continued reading. Against all odds the fictional family started pulling together, and all but one of the family members survived. I finished the book before going up to bed. All in all, it was a very quiet day.

2,623 STEPS TODAY

THE MAN WITH THE YELLOW ARROW
FRIDAY, JULY 8, 2016
LAS HERRERIAS TO O'CEBREIRO
DAY 38

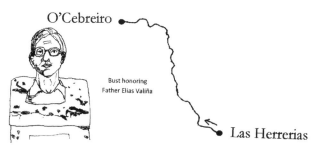

O'Cebreiro

Bust honoring
Father Elias Valiña

Las Herrerias

After breakfast, I settled down to work on catching up on my blog posts. The WiFi wasn't very good, and I found it very frustrating. I couldn't get anything to upload. I gave up after a while. I have my travel journal, and so long as I keep that up to date I can always catch up on the blog when I arrive somewhere with good WiFi.

After lunch, we took a taxi to our next stop on the Camino, O'Cebreiro. This is a very old, tiny, quite famous village, thanks to a miracle that supposedly took place here. Michener wrote about it; he had a wonderful, mysterious, and somewhat scary experience here.

O'Cebreiro is also the highest point along the Camino. I'm glad I didn't have to climb the hill to get up here but instead was able to ride on four wheels in comfort. Not a very pilgrim-like thing to say, but the truth. *The spirit is willing but the flesh is weak.*

At the hotel, I was very disappointed to find out that there was no WiFi whatsoever. What a bummer! To assuage my resulting bad temper, I went out to visit the local church, Santa Maria la Real.

Santa Maria is supposed to be the oldest church on the Camino, dating all the way back to the ninth century, when pilgrims first starting trekking to Santiago. The church is very simple and plain, but beautiful. I bought a postcard of its huge twelfth century baptismal font. By the looks of it, new Christians got a full immersion in the baptismal water rather than just a sprinkling of water on the forehead.

I wandered into the side garden where busts and plaques honoring Father Elías Valiña, the Spanish priest who re-popularized the Camino in the 1970s, have been placed by Camino associations from around the world. (See Chapter 21, "Father Elías Valiña," on page 108.)

I searched for a plaque, or memorial stone, or other monument from APOC, but could not find one. Back at the church, I asked the clerk on duty at the small shop selling religious items whether there was something from America in the garden.

"No, there isn't," she said.

"Why not?" I asked. "Americans make up the largest national contingent walking the Camino. We should be represented."

"I don't know," she replied.

"If APOC offered a plaque for hanging on the wall, would it be welcome?"

"Of course. As you can see, we have items from all over the world."

It made me sad that we Americans had failed to offer homage to this remarkable man. I'm going to ask my Houston chapter leaders why not, and maybe post a query on the APOC website.

James says we are eating too much. He's right. On days when we walk a lot, eating big meals is fine, but on days like this one when we are mostly physically inactive, we need to cut back. We decided to skip dinner.

3,793 STEPS TODAY

THE SHEPHERD'S MIRACLE
SATURDAY, JULY 9, 2016
O'CEBREIRO TO TRICASTELA
DAY 39

James had no interest, given his bad foot, in walking around O'Cebreiro, with its rough paving stones, so I set off alone to explore. I went back to the church, this time to see again the chalice and paten that are at the heart of the famous miracle. I won't go into the details. (Michener tells it much better than I could, having heard the tale from a local shepherd on a dark and stormy night.)

The basic story is that a priest based in this town during the Middle Ages resented during the long snowed-in winters having to leave his warm hearth in order to say mass each day in this very cold church for a single parishioner, a humble shepherd. You can probably guess what happens and how the priest gets his just deserts. It's a lovely tale.

As I have throughout this journey whenever I have been in a church, I dropped to my knees and said an Our Father, a Hail Mary, a thank you to my mother and father, and a special plea to my sister, my own Saint Muffet, for her intercession. If anyone in heaven can help me and the rest of my family, it is she.

I also requested the help of Saint James. Besides being the patron saint of Spain and the reason for the existence of this pilgrimage route, St James is the namesake and hence patron saint of my uncle, my brother, my ex-husband, my ex-father-in-law, my son, and my nephew. "James" has special meaning on both sides of my family. I purchased a prayer card with a prayer to Saint James, and I silently recited it before leaving the church.

I went to the Palloza Museum next. O'Cebreiro is an ancient hill town, and the museum was filled with artifacts from bygone eras. It was interesting to learn how these hill people lived in their low slung *pallozas* (cottages) that look to me like brown mushrooms with thatch caps.

This town has really changed since Michener was here in the late 1960s, when it was practically a ghost town. Pilgrims have revived it. It now has several hostels and at least two gift shops catering to the visitors. As usual, I ducked into the tourist shops to see what treasures I could find. I purchased an O'Cebreiro pin to add to the collection of pins I have been amassing, one for each town in which we stop.

James and I set out for Tricastela in a taxi. We are booked into an amazing complex for pilgrims. Most of the rooms are dormitory style, but we have a private room with bath. Best of all, the complex boasts a laundry and WiFi. While washing clothes, I caught up on email and news from home. There is bad news out of Dallas. Three policemen have been killed in what might be the start of some sort of revenge killings for the murders of black men by policemen.

6,684 STEPS TODAY

A King's Lodging
Sunday, July 10, 2016
Tricastela to Sarria
Day 40

Sarria

Tricastela

Another taxi, this time from Tricastela to Sarria.

We are staying in the only high-end hotel of this trip, the four-star Hotel Alfonso IX. Once checked in, we enjoyed the hotel's fluffy towels and commodious bathroom, a huge step up from the modest arrangements of our previous lodgings.

I headed out for a 7:30 pm pilgrims' mass, which was held at a very small church. There were more pilgrims here than I had seen in days. I stopped in at a larger church, Santa Marina, on the way to the pilgrims' mass in order to ask for my Sarria *sello* (stamp) for my Camino passport.

James met me for dinner. We had a lovely tapas meal, accompanied by sangria. Nothing better, to my way of thinking.

On the way back to the hotel, we came across a youth group that was singing in a plaza. We had seen the same group in Tricastela, but hadn't realized they were a choral group. We listened to them for a while, with James offering musical commentary, before heading back to our hotel.

7,162 steps today

LAST REST STOP
MONDAY, JULY 11, 2016
SARRIA
DAY 41

Sarria

This is our last rest day before our final push to Santiago de Compostela. We spent the bulk of the day doing chores, with me writing in my journal and reading about this part of the Camino while our clothes dried. We lunched in the hotel cafeteria, having salad and octopus. Yummy. Just the sort of light lunch we wanted.

James wished to see the two churches I had visited the night before. We walked up to St. Marina, where a pilgrims' mass was almost over. I went to communion even though I felt guilty for missing most of the service. A guitarist and a group of singers filled the church with music.

I found a shop that was still open and purchased my Sarria pin, which was in the shape of a tiny pilgrim.

Wanting a change from the usual Spanish menu, we went to an Italian restaurant for dinner. There was a very boisterous table of pilgrims from a variety of countries—Koreans, Americans, and so forth. They were celebrating someone's birthday. James began playing his guitar, which he had brought along. The Koreans snapped a photo of us and immediately printed it on some sort of new technology they had. Cool. Sort of like an updated Polaroid camera, dispensing photos immediately, but very small ones.

4,814 STEPS TODAY

STUBBED TOES AND SKIDDING!
TUESDAY, JULY 12, 2016
SARRIA TO PORTOMARIN
DAY 42

Portomarin

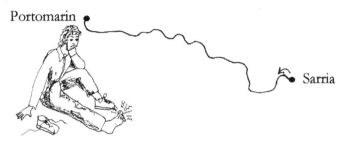

Sarria

We are now on the final days of our pilgrimage. From Sarria to Santiago is 100 kilometers, the minimum required distance to walk in order to qualify for a Compostela. As a result, many pilgrims start their pilgrimage at Sarria, and the Camino will be full of pilgrims.

This was going to be a long walk. Despite his foot, James was determined to do it so as to qualify for his Compostela. We were up at 6:00 am, downstairs for breakfast by 7:00 am, and out the hotel door by 8:00 am.

It was a fairly good surface, but uphill, uphill, uphill, which I abhor. We stopped for drinks, and then stopped again for lunch. Boots off, sweaty feet recovering from the slog. After lunch, off again for another ten kilometers. In total, we had to walk twenty-three kilometers. And once we made it to Portomarin, we still had to go another 0.8 kilometers from the center of the town to our hotel, not counting the steps we wasted because we couldn't find the hotel and wandered in circles for a while.

While the road was basically OK, there were a lot of buried rocks, with just their tops peeking out. Since I tend to shuffle along, I stubbed my toes at least six times. (Thanks, Keens, for protecting my toes.) And I skidded once. (Thanks, walking poles, for stabilizing me.) The final descent into Portomarin was horrible, as bad as or worse than the descent into Zubiri.

42,678 STEPS TODAY

STALKED BY A FAMILIAR
WEDNESDAY, JULY 13, 2016
PORTOMARIN TO PALAS DE REI
DAY 43

Today is July 13. My brother, named but never called James, will be celebrating his birthday back home.

This was another hard day of walking—twenty-three kilometers! The day was quite cool, and there was shade along the way. Still, the path was up and down, up and down, which is hard for a flatlander like me.

I finally arrived at Palas de Rei around 6:00 pm, totally knackered, my feet hurting. I wasn't sure I could even walk another step in order to go to dinner, but at 9:40 pm I finally levered myself up off the bed and we walked several blocks from the hotel to the restaurant. Outside, besides being cool there was a strong wind. We are still at a high elevation. I broke out my jacket for the first time in many days and was glad to have it.

We just made it to the restaurant before closing time. We had to rush in to place an order before the place's announced 10:00 pm closing time. We had a very nice waiter who obviously saw that we were all done in. He gave us a couple of free soft drinks after he saw how thirsty we were, and then hot chocolate after the meal.

On the way back to the hotel, a Siamese cat followed us for blocks. James, as he had many times on the Camino, again wished we had a pet waiting for us back home. (Our last cat had died and not been replaced.)

49,723 STEPS TODAY

BASTILLE DAY ON THE FRENCH ROUTE
THURSDAY, JULY 14, 2016
PALAS DE REI TO MELIDE
DAY 44

Bastille Day. I'll have to remember to congratulate any French pilgrims I encounter.

Walking, walking, walking, but with frequent stops for cold soft drinks and then for lunch. Very slow going, overall.

Earlier along the Camino we sometimes went a full day hardly seeing anyone. Now, the streams of pilgrims from various routes, plus all the new pilgrims who started at Sarria, are joining together for the final push into Santiago. The trickle of people has become a river.

With so many more people along the Camino than was true previously, we had more occasions to talk to others. We met a group of six American Episcopalians from New Jersey. Two had already walked from Sarria to Santiago once before. We also chatted with a couple of other groups.

A wonderful experience occurred along the route. There are many high school groups walking this *stage* of the Camino. They are all faster walkers than I am, so I hear them approaching from behind, chatting and giggling. Eventually they catch up with me, pass me, then speed ahead.

Once, I heard a group far back singing, though I couldn't distinguish the tunes. As they got closer, I realized they were singing Beatles tunes. As they passed me, I saw a number of them holding their telephones in their hands, the song lyrics displayed on their screens. How great to hear a group of Spanish high school girls on a religious route singing in accented English "Help," "Let It Be," and "Hey, Jude."

We stopped at a church along the way, following my rule never to pass up an open church. It was called San Xulian (St. Julian). There I had an interesting conversation with the man staffing the church. He was a lay missionary in an organization that was founded by an Italian. Mostly the group does its missionary work in Africa, but they also go to Latin America. Now they are trying to get the churches along the Camino open (Hurray!) by offering to staff them.

It sounded like a very interesting group, and I heartily support getting more churches open for pilgrims. I put a slightly larger-than-usual donation in the box.

29,112 STEPS TODAY

STARTING AT YOUR FRONT DOOR
FRIDAY, JULY 15, 2016
MELIDE TO ARZUA
DAY 45

James's foot was really bothering him, so we went to two pharmacies to find more foot rub and perhaps new boot inserts. It was after 10:00 am before I could set off down the Camino, a very hot day.

I encountered several groups I had met previously: the six Americans from New Jersey, for example, and the three Filipinos, one of them a priest, we had seen at dinner the previous night. I chatted briefly with them all.

The most interesting conversation I had was with an American woman from California. She took seriously the old pilgrimage method in which a pilgrim began her journey when she stepped outside her front door headed for Santiago.

Instead of starting in Saint-Jean-Pied-de-Port, or Sarria, or some other famous jumping off spot, she began in California. She exited her front door a pilgrim and took three days to walk to LAX airport. She did have to take a plane across the ocean, but otherwise it was walking all the way. She gave me a handmade cloth rosary.

When I made it to Arzua, I was very hot and sweaty. The last six kilometers had been particularly rough. I was too tired to seek out a laundromat, but I needed some clean clothes. I turned a few things over to the hotel receptionist to have washed.

There was a fiesta in Arzua. Two bands struck up at 10:30 pm and played until 4:00 am. Heavy traffic roared by the pension at which we stayed. I found it hard to sleep.

30,922 STEPS TODAY

Why Didn't I Stop?
Saturday, July 16, 2016
Arzua to Pedrouzo
Day 46

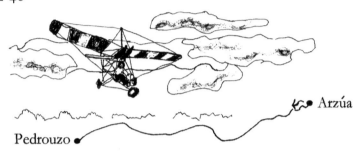

I'm afraid I've gotten into the "I want to finish this" mindset. Two days to go until Santiago, and I am ready to do something besides walking for the sake of walking. Truthfully, I found this stretch of the Camino very boring, with little to see. But maybe it isn't boring, maybe my mind is just so focused on getting to Santiago that I have become like others who rush past everything in their hurry to get where they are going.

I saw the six Americans again and the three Filipinos. We exchanged *"Buen Caminos"* in passing. Early in the morning I saw three nuns who were giving passersby a stamp and talking to them. I already had my stamp for the day, so I didn't stop. I regretted it later. I also walked right by a church and didn't even check to see if it was open. I was too anxious to walk as far as possible before it got too hot.

The road was fairly good, though there was shale. The temperature rose throughout the day until it was scorching.

The only interesting thing I saw was an ultralight aircraft with a man suspended below the wings. I wondered where he came from, and whether there was some sort of commercial concession around to take advantage of all the visitors, like the parasailing you see at beaches.

At dinner, James and I celebrated our last night on the Camino.

35,247 STEPS TODAY

LAST SPRINT
SUNDAY, JULY 17, 2016
PEDROUZO TO SANTIAGO
DAY 47

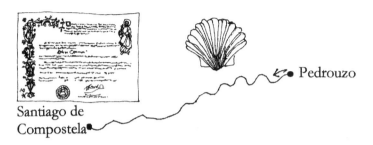

Santiago de
Compostela

Pedrouzo

Up early to start the final day of walking. I wanted to avoid the heat as much as possible and get to Santiago as early as I could. The weather forecast said it was going to get up to 100 degrees today. I didn't even stop for lunch, though I did grab a cold drink at mid-morning.

I don't remember much about the walk other than the relief of finally walking into Santiago. I was heading for the main plaza when who should rush out of a restaurant but our Romanian journalist friend. We hadn't seen her for weeks, and then suddenly there she was. She said she saw us coming up the street from her seat by the large picture window. She had made it to Santiago several days previously and was winding up her Camino broadcasts. We hugged, and made plans to meet later for drinks.

Later in the afternoon, James and I went to the office dispensing Compostelas. I only took my second Camino passport, not realizing that there was an advantage to taking both. (Having completely filled up one passport with stamps, I purchased a second one about a month into our pilgrimage.) As a result, my Compostela just records the 100 kilometers I walked from Sarria to Santiago, not the whole distance I had walked from Saint-Jean-Pied-de-Port.

James and I later went to the appointed meeting place, but our Romanian friend did not appear. It was fine. There was a lot going on in Santiago. We ran into the New Jersey Six, and all of us high-fived at having completed our pilgrimage. Dinner was a celebration, with two kinds of sangria. After dinner, we came across some street musicians playing Galician bagpipes and stopped to listen. Of course, we further celebrated while listening by ordering an after-dinner drink.

40,470 STEPS TODAY

On the Plaza
Monday, July 18, 2016
Santiago de Compostela
Day 48

Santiago de Compostela

A day to savor Santiago. After breakfast, we went shopping. I bought a ceramic statue of St. James wearing pilgrim attire. I really like it, but of course buying a ceramic item is crazy. I'll be lucky to get it home unbroken. I also purchased a number of small souvenir items for gifts back home.

Mass was at noon at the cathedral. I had asked if the famous Santiago Botafumeiro (a thurible, which is a censer that releases incense) was going to swing at any time on Monday or Tuesday. There doesn't seem to be a regular schedule for the Botafumeiro.

One of the cathedral assistants told me that some groups pay to have the Botafumeiro swing, but such times are unpredictable. Lucky pilgrims just happen to be in the cathedral at the right time. I wasn't lucky. The assistant suggested that I try again the following morning. There was a large number of African pilgrims in the cathedral, including a youth chorus that sang during mass.

We ate lunch at a café right on the cathedral square. I had sangria and read my book. A guitarist strummed and sang. James went to speak with him and to examine his guitar. This is what I love: sitting in a Spanish plaza with a beautiful view before me (the cathedral and all the activity on the square), with a jug of sangria and a good book. Heaven. The pilgrims arriving at the cathedral—journey's end—were all joyous, taking photos and embracing and laughing.

St. James awaited us. When the pilgrim rush thinned out, we went into the cathedral and got in the queue to hug the statue of St. James and see the crypt and tomb where the saint rests.

After paying our respects to St. James, I did a bit more light shopping, then back to the square to listen to music and watch people. A delightful day.

9,986 STEPS TODAY

LAND'S END
TUESDAY, JULY 19, 2016
SANTIAGO DE COMPOSTELA TO FINISTERRE TO SANTIAGO
DAY 49

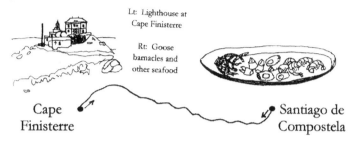

Lt: Lighthouse at Cape Finisterre

Rt: Goose barnacles and other seafood

Cape Finisterre

Santiago de Compostela

Many pilgrims, having arrived in Santiago, continue on to Finisterre (Land's End). Some walk there, but James and I took a bus.

We had wasted time after breakfast by going to the Pilgrim's Office to see if we could purchase discount train tickets to Madrid (we couldn't), so we felt pressed for time.

By express bus the trip to Finisterre was an hour and a half. I had proposed to James that we perform a time-honored pilgrim custom: burn a set of worn-out Camino clothes on the beach. Judging by the raggedy clothes I had seen drying on lines along the Camino, many peoples' clothes deserved to be burned. We didn't have any "holey" clothes, so James declined burning anything.

At a seafood restaurant, I finally found *percebes* (barnacles) on the menu. I had searched for them all along the Camino, but this was the first restaurant to offer them. I first had a taste of these salty sea delights years ago in Portugal, and I hungered for them. They were every bit as good, though a lot more expensive, than the ones I remembered from Portugal.

We took advantage of the restaurant's specialties and also had octopus and seafood paella, plus *cava* (Spanish sparkling wine), all of which we shared. This meal was another splurge to celebrate having gone to the ends of the earth on this journey.

After our late lunch we walked out to the lighthouse and tossed pebbles into the Atlantic. I thought of the rock I had left behind at the Iron Cross, and tucked a pebble into my pocket. We took photos, had a quick look around an exhibit, and purchased a couple of Finisterre souvenirs, such as a lighthouse bottle opener. (How could anyone pass that up? Too unique!)

We raced back to the bus station to catch the 7:00 pm express to Santiago.

9,150 STEPS TODAY

I finally got to eat percebes in Finisterre. They don't look like much, but they taste of the sea and are delicious.

My son and I end our journey as we began it, together, with our daypacks on. Celebrating, but a little sad too. At least from now on, St. James has our backs!

ON TO MADRID
WEDNESDAY, JULY 20, 2016
SANTIAGO DE COMPOSTELA TO MADRID
DAY 50

Santiago de
Compostela

Madrid

This was our last day as pilgrims. We weren't leaving Spain yet—we still had stops in Madrid and Toledo planned—but we would be transitioning from pilgrims to tourists. I wanted to take advantage of these last few hours of the trip that I had thought about, and planned for, for such a long time.

I went back to the cathedral and spent some quiet time in prayer. Then out to the plaza to buy a few things I had spied the previous day but had not purchased. The most significant was a resin statue of St. James as a pilgrim. I had seen it and liked it the previous day, but finally opted for the ceramic St. James.

Over the previous night, I worried that the ceramic version wouldn't survive the trip home, besides which I liked both statues. So I bought the resin one too. Mentally I placed them in my home: one in my bedroom, overlooking me as I slept, and one in my living room, where it could be admired by my visitors.

Because the shop check-out process went slowly, I had to sprint back to the cathedral to catch the 10:30 am mass in English. James met me there, but spent his time looking around the cathedral rather than following the mass.

After mass, we went back to the hotel to pack our bags and check out, and then caught a taxi to the train station. Adios, Santiago. I'll be back sometime, I'm sure. Once is not enough.

12,203 STEPS TODAY

Chapter 24
Madrid and Toledo

NO MATTER WHAT YOUR TIME LIMITATIONS are, I strongly suggest that you reserve a few days at the end of your journey to visit Madrid and Toledo. These two cultural meccas are not to be missed, and add another, very different dimension to your Spanish journey.

Madrid is the country's political, intellectual, and cultural capital, and is moreover stunningly beautiful. Its numerous plazas, fountains, and magnificent government buildings give it a grandeur that, for me, always recalls to my mind, more than any other city, the architectural glories of Washington, DC. While DC is gleaming white marble, Madrid is cream or gold-toned multistoried buildings built around very large plazas. I can't move through those spaces without recalling that in the 16th century Madrid was the DC of its time, the capital of a great, sprawling empire in control of large swaths of the world.

Our travel to and from the Camino was through Madrid's airport, and so I had built into our schedule a week in Madrid at the end of our trip. After our pilgrimage, my son and I were tired, so we took it fairly easy this last week in Spain. One day while in Madrid we bought tickets for a hop-on-hop-off bus tour line. We rode a whole route, then switched and rode the other route, just taking in the sights and sounds of urban Madrid, so different from the small, quiet, almost deserted villages of northern Spain.

For me, the magnificence of Madrid resides in its museums. First and foremost, of course, is the Prado. I first visited the Prado, one of the greatest art museums in the world, when I was twenty-one. I had never experienced anything like it. I remember going to the area housing Diego Velazquez's paintings and seeing *Las Meninas*, a portrait of the royal court of Philip IV of Spain. In high school, my Spanish teacher had two Velazquez prints on her classroom walls, one of the painting *The Lancers*, or *The Surrender of Breda*, and the other of a Spanish prince astride a very fat little pony with a flowing mane. I remember dreaming away hot afternoons in Miss Fink's classroom, looking at the two Velazquez prints when I should have been trying to conjugate Spanish verbs.

Once at the Prado, all those many years ago, I knew I had to head for Diego Velazquez. I found *The Lancers* and the painting with the prince and the fat pony, but it was *Las Meninas* (the Maids of Honor) that entranced me. This was not a mighty military scene, like *The Lancers*, or a portrait of a king-to-be, like the prince on his pony. This was a family scene, with a golden-haired princess front and center, while her two maids of honor attend her. Sharing the foreground of the painting are a dog and two dwarfs, while the images of the princess's parents, Philip IV and his queen Mariana of Austria, appear in a mirror located on the far back wall of this painted, two-dimensional room. Meanwhile, the viewer can see Velazquez himself behind a giant canvas, with his paintbrush in hand. Given the placement of the figures, Velazquez is actually painting Philip IV and his queen (who are standing more or less where the viewer stands and whose images are reflected in the mirror on the back wall) rather than the scene we viewers see—the princess, the maids of honor, the dwarfs, and the dog. A delight to the mind (since it is a puzzle to solve) and to the eye (with the delicate laces and shimmery materials of the girls' clothing), this painting is a feast that can be consumed over many visits.

I also remember in those long-ago days seeing Hieronymus Bosch's *The Garden of Earthly Delights* and being equal parts attracted and repulsed by the strange and mysterious images of saints, sinners, and phantasmagorical creatures. And I know I visited Francisco de Goya's paintings, but found them too dark and depressing for my taste. On that long-ago visit, I spent the whole day in the Prado and left knowing that I had just scratched the surface of the museum.

It was one of my pleasures at the end of the Camino trip to be able to take my son James to the Prado for his first visit. As it happens, he already knew and liked Bosch, so we decided to visit that area first. We were extremely lucky; there was a special Bosch exhibit at the Prado. It took us half a day just to wend our way through the numerous Bosch paintings, each a testament to a mind that seemed to have an unlimited ability to imagine what has never existed.

After Bosch, my son and I split up, each to visit our chosen painters. Of course, I made my way to *Las Meninas*, and delighted once again in the *Infanta* (princess) Margarita, with her flowing blond hair and beautiful court dress. This is probably my favorite painting in the whole world, and I never tire of it. Also entranced by the other paintings of royals, I moved on to see the portraits of Philip IV—anything but handsome with his long jaw and narrow face—and his queen Mariana of Austria—who is no beauty either.

While I don't like Goya's military paintings or his dark, end-of-life works, I have come to love and appreciate his two *Maja* paintings. In the *Majas*, the same woman reclines on a chaise lounge, with her hands behind her head. In one of the portraits, she is clothed, and in the other nude. The woman is supposedly the Duchess of Alba, who kept these two paintings in her private dressing room, from which they only emerged after her death. This was the era of the Spanish Inquisition, whose inquisitors did not countenance nudity, so it took artistic courage to paint the *Maja Desnuda*. Ever since Goya's time, painter after painter has offered up his own version of the clothed or nude *Maja*, and I can never see such a reclining figure without thinking about the Prado and recalling the two Goya *Majas*. I wanted James to see and savor the *Majas*, and he did.

The Prado is just one of the many magnificent museums in Madrid. On another day, James and I made our way to the Reina Sofia Museum, which houses paintings from the twentieth century. Spain, of course, is the homeland of Picasso, Dali, Miro, Gris, and many other famous modern painters. James particularly likes Dali, so we visited his paintings first, before strolling through other galleries.

To me, it is always a bit of a shock to see American painters like Warhol in a Spanish art museum. In the Prado, the painters whose works are shown are overwhelmingly Spanish—either Spanish born, like Velazquez and Goya, or painters who came from the Spanish empire, like Rubens. That all of these painters flocked to the Spanish court to seek royal patronage gives visitors a better insight into the power, size, and influence of Spain in the fifteenth to nineteenth centuries than any history book can.

The Reina Sofia has a different atmosphere than the Prado. Yes, Spanish painters still dominate the museum and are clear leaders in the art world, particularly in the early 1900s, but Spain itself is no longer the colossus it once was. History has moved on. Pop art is American, not Spanish. Warhol's quartered portrait of Billy Idol hangs there, sharing a venue with Picasso's magnificent *Guernica*, which is surely the most famous anti-war painting ever done.

In the Reina Sofia, I particularly love seeing the paintings of women in elegant dresses. Usually duchesses, but sometimes just plain mistresses, these women glow off the canvas and whisper of bygone elegance and beauty. They make me long to have a portrait of myself painted, though I am neither a duchess nor famous nor beautiful. Maybe my painter can lie, or maybe he can transform dross into gold. In any case, I long to figure in that line of women marching through art history.

There are many other worthy museums in Madrid, but the Prado and the Reina Sofia reign supreme. James and I also visited royal palaces and armories and other wonderous spots in Madrid, but the Prado and the Reina Sofia are the jewels in the Spanish crown.

The second not-to-be missed town that I recommend you go to is Toledo, which is an easy day trip from Madrid. If possible, stay overnight there; you won't regret it. In Toledo, of all Spanish cities, you can best experience the confluence of the Spanish, Muslim, and Jewish cultures, as those communities lived peacefully in Toledo for very long periods.

Toledo was the political capital of Spain until 1561, when the king moved the capital to Madrid. As the seat of the ruling families for periods throughout the ages, Toledo naturally was the cultural and spiritual capital as well as being its center of government. Among Toledo's famous artists was the painter El Greco (the Greek). His elongated figures in the numerous paintings you can see in Toledo are a unique and easily recognizable style. A visit to Santo Tomé, the church housing El Greco's masterpiece *The Burial of Count Orgaz*, is a required stop for all art lovers. There is, of course, the El Greco Museum in Toledo, well worth the time it takes to visit. Soaked in dark spirituality, El Greco's paintings give a glimpse into a mindset that is so far from our own twenty-first century world view that it is almost impossible to fathom. But if we try to put ourselves into the world of those paintings, we can better understand how thousands and thousands of pilgrims walked out of their homes each year and began the long trek to Santiago de Compostela, a journey from which many of them never returned.

Toledo was (and is) the home of the famous Toledo steel blades, renowned in earlier times as being made from the finest forged metal there was. Prized by knights from around the world, these Toledo blades allowed those owning them to go into battle secure in the knowledge that their blades were stronger than any others then existing and were capable of breaking their opponent's weapons. Thinking about the importance of a superior fighting weapon for Spanish soldiers during the reconquest of Spain in the late fifteenth century and the conquest of the New World in the sixteenth also helps us understand the zeitgeist of the age. In today's Toledo, you can still visit small *talleres* (workshops) turning out replica weapons and other items, forged with Toledo steel.

Walking around Toledo, particularly at night, can make you feel as though you've caught a time machine back to an earlier era. Its ancient walls, castle, arched gateways, labyrinthian streets, and hidden-away gardens all whisper of an earlier time and give me an overwhelming feeling of déjà vu.

Toledo was also the scene of one of the most dramatic and difficult battles of the Spanish Civil War, the Siege of the Alcazar. If you have time, it is very worthwhile to learn more about how Spain in the late 1930s tore itself apart, in a war I'd characterize as even more vicious and bloody than our own American Civil War. Men on the wrong side were summarily taken out and shot, and Germany, on the side of the fascist Nationalists led by Generalissimo Francisco Franco, experimented in Spain with its newly developed weapons on a population with no defenses. Picasso's famous painting *Guernica* depicts one of the resulting massacres.

Michener talks a lot about the Spanish Civil War in *Iberia*, and at Toledo's Alcazar fortress the Nationalists—the bad guys in the eyes of most Americans—held out against starvation, artillery, bombing from the air, sickness, and every other horror until finally Franco's troops broke through Republican lines to relieve the besieged Nationalists. When I walk the ramparts where defenders held out so long against the odds, I seem to hear distant bugles, an echo of that terrible war.

* * *

The Camino was important for European Christians for hundreds of years, but it became peripheral to the life of Spain and the world as time moved on. By the early twentieth century, it was dying. It has now been resurrected, but there is little that is modern along the Camino except for the bigger cities. To experience the reality of present-day Spain and its history over the last few hundred years, short visits to Madrid and Toledo at the end of your Camino adventure will take you out of the medieval period and firmly ground you in the Spain of today—no longer an empire, but still an exciting and interesting place to visit and a banquet for art lovers.

Chapter 25
A Letter to the Relevant Spanish Ministers

A S I WALKED ALONG THE CAMINO, thinking about food, my feet, how much longer I had to walk that day, and so forth, I would also think about how the Government of Spain could make the Camino experience *better* for pilgrims. I spent thirty-three years in government, so it is not surprising that I think about how governments can improve matters. I thought about all sorts of governmental areas of responsibility, from installing benches at appropriate spots along the Camino to making the Camino more accessible to people who can't walk it. When I got home, I composed the following letter to send to the relevant ministries. There doesn't seem to be one Spanish federal-level ministry in overall charge of the Camino, so the letter is directed to the various ministries that could make a difference.

I did not send the letter right away. I put it aside, wondering whether it would be worthwhile to send it. Would it even reach the ministers to whom it is addressed? Would it elicit a thoughtful reply, or possibly raise hackles? After a while, I shared a draft with some other writers, asking them questions about the letter. Did it strike the tone for which I was aiming? If you were a minister and you received a letter like this, would it make you angry or make you think? After all, the goal is not to criticize but to encourage further improvement and development of the Camino.

After hearing the writers' answers, I put the letter aside again, thinking some more about whether sending it would be just another example of my hubris. Finally, I asked myself the question, "What would Father Elías do?" and so decided to mail it. As I say in the letter, if I receive a reply from any of the ministers, I will post it on my blog.

October 23, 2019

The Honorable
José Guirao Cabrera
Minister of Culture and Sport
Government of Spain
Casa de las Sietes Chimeneas
Plaza del Rey, 1
28004 Madrid, Spain

The Honorable
María Reyes Maroto Illera
Minister of Industry, Trade and Tourism
Paseo de la Castellana, 160
28046 Madrid, Spain

The Honorable
José Luis Ábalos Meco
Minister of Development
Paseo de la Castellana, 67
28071 Madrid, Spain

Dear Ministers Guirao, Maroto, and Ábalos:

First, please let me introduce myself. I am a retired United States diplomat. From 1992-1994, I was the desk officer in the United States Information Agency in Washington, DC, responsible for coordinating certain relations with Spain. I first visited Spain in 1972, and I taught English in Barcelona in 1974. My love of Spain has continued throughout my life, and in 2016 I achieved a dream I had held for some forty years when I was able to travel the Camino de Santiago from Saint-Jean-Pied-de-Port in France all the way to Santiago de Compostela.

My letter to you today is about the Camino. I am now finishing up a book about my walk along the Camino, and I plan to publish this open letter in my book, along with any response you may choose to send me.

Please understand that the remarks below come from a sincere friend of Spain and the Camino. I believe that, in having the Camino, Spain possesses a jewel of great value.

However, I do not believe that the Camino is currently receiving the support of the Government of Spain that it merits.

First, as far as I can discern, there is no Ministry that bears overall responsibility for the Camino. I have contacted the Consulate of Spain here in Houston, and the first response that I received was that there is no federal body responsible for the Camino. Rather, I was told that the individual provincial governments through which the Camino passes are responsible for the Camino. As a citizen of a decentralized country, I certainly understand the idea that states or provinces should be responsible for their areas. However, in my government, and I believe in yours, there is also a recognition that when matters cross state or provincial lines, be the matter commerce or transport or other issues, there is a federal responsibility as well.

The second response I received from the Consulate pointed me towards federations of Camino friends (particularly in France), the EU Consejo, and the Galician provincial government—but no Spanish ministry.

While acknowledging that my knowledge of the organization of the Government of Spain is very limited, it would seem to me that your ministries—Culture, Tourism, and

Development—all have a role to play in publicizing, promoting, developing, and protecting the Camino. I have therefore addressed this letter to all of you.

Some observations I made along the Camino, and my suggestions, follow.

1) As I mentioned above, I believe that the Camino is a jewel of Spain. It combines history, culture, adventure, and spiritual growth all into one package. It attracts thousands of tourists from many countries. It is revitalizing a part of Spain that was suffering from outward migration, reviving towns along the Camino that were virtual ghost towns before pilgrims began pouring through them in route to Santiago. Despite this, I saw little evidence of governmental support for the Camino as I walked along it. I believe that your ministries, each of them, could play a vital role in turning this around.

2) **Transport**. In places, the Camino is in very poor repair, and is even dangerous. I myself was in fear more than once of slipping and falling and having a serious injury. Along the whole Camino, I only came across one stretch where a road crew was working on the Camino. Right now, the Camino is mostly a destination for younger and healthy travelers, but that could change if infrastructure for older and handicapped travelers is put in place. Ministry assistance in ensuring that the most dangerous sections are fixed would be a huge positive development. Also, Ministry assistance in developing alternate routes for the most difficult patches along the way would be wonderful.

3) **Transport**. I traveled along the Camino with my son, who injured his foot while walking. Thereafter, he had to take buses or taxis to our next stops along the Camino. I was quite surprised to find that many of the towns along the Camino are not linked either by bus or train, making hiring a taxi the only way to

progress to the next stopping point. I believe that establishing bus routes all along the Camino would ensure that more pilgrims, especially those who are mobility challenged, could experience the Camino. Knowing that public transport is available would also attract travelers who want to travel the Camino, but not necessarily on foot. Ministry assistance in funding minibus transportation along the whole Camino would be an extremely positive development.

4) **Culture.** I was continually surprised along the Camino by how many churches were closed and unavailable to visit. Even those that did open usually had limited hours. For those of us who love history and culture, having an opportunity to visit those historic churches would add to our trip. Ministry assistance in supporting hours for visits to churches would help pilgrims to slow down and appreciate the culture, history, and art of Spain.

5) **Tourism.** With so many pilgrims traveling through northern Spain along the Camino, the Ministry could assist by making certain that facilities for up-market pilgrims are also available and publicized. There are many organizations and groups that distribute information about how to walk along the Camino and stay in albergues, but there is less assistance in planning a Camino visit that does not involve exclusively walking or staying in hostels. In my own case, I went to an Irish organization for help in booking small hotels, bed and breakfast lodgings, and the like. I would have preferred to give my business to a Spanish company or organization, but I did not find one. The Ministry could assist by supporting more information for pilgrims who want to visit, but who are not budget travelers only wanting to stay in the hostels.

6) **Tourism.** More information for travelers who want to savor Spain, its culture, history, and art, would be very helpful along the Camino. For example, a calendar of events designed

specifically for pilgrims, informing visitors well in advance—when they are planning their trips—about major festivals and events along the way, would be wonderful. Several times along the Camino, I learned that I had just missed a festival in a town. Had I known about it in advance, I could have adjusted dates to be there to attend the festival. Similarly, some sort of signage along the Camino informing pilgrims about important sites or major events in the neighborhood would be spectacular. For example, historical markers along the way, or signs guiding pilgrims to nearby museums or art galleries, would be a boon to visitors. I observed many pilgrims rushing from one point to another, not stopping to drink in the culture around them. Easily accessible information posted along the Camino could aid those pilgrims to slow down and savor Spain.

7) **Development**. With pilgrims pouring into northern Spain, your ministries could play a vital role in coordinating support for the Camino among all the federal ministries and provincial governments. It should be easy for pilgrims to figure out how to contact the relevant ministry about the Camino, but right now it is difficult.

8) **Development**. There should be "one-stop-shopping" in some governmental office that potential pilgrims could contact for information. I have searched around the Internet, but I have not found any such Spanish governmental site. A pilgrim might have questions about many different topics—Is there a bus between points A and B? What are the best towns in which to shop for a Spanish guitar? What fruits and vegetables are in season in Spain in August? An office that could easily and quickly respond to such questions, without making the visitor who is planning a trip hunt around for the information, would be very valuable.

Gentlemen, thank you for your attention. I hope you understand that I am offering these suggestions because of my love of

Spain and my appreciation of the Camino. I believe that much more can and should be done to improve the Camino, for the benefit of Spain and for all of the visitors to the Camino.

As I mentioned above, I plan to publish this letter in my book, along with your replies, should you favor me with one.

Sincerely,

[Signed]
Julie Gianelloni Connor
Senior U.S. Foreign Service Officer (ret.)
Owner and Editor, Bayou City Press

Chapter 26
Deep Thoughts

BEFORE I WENT ON THE CAMINO, I read a number of books by other pilgrims. I was struck by how many of them—all of them, really—reported having some sort of deep, spiritual revelation or experience along the way.

I fully expected that I, too, would have such Deep Thoughts along my journey. During a period in my adolescence, I was quite religious, and even thought I might have a religious vocation. That period did not last long, and I don't consider myself religious now, but I do still think a religious grounding is a good thing. I still believe that religion and religious organizations are, on the whole, positive, and I tried to give my son that grounding and that feeling of community that participation in weekly religious services can offer.

As I walked along, I thought about various things.

One thing I kept thinking about was my house. After my retirement, I moved into a wonderful house. I am so grateful to the previous owners, who did all the work of expanding and modernizing it. Before choosing a retirement home to purchase, I had made a list of all the characteristics I wanted in my retirement home, and the house I bought had all of those characteristics. After having lived in the house for two years, though, I had gradually come to realize that the house, while wonderful, was not quite perfect. It could stand a few alterations.

It has no covered, screened porch or patio, and there are times, particularly early mornings and at twilight, when I would like to sit outside and read, without having to worry about sunburn or mosquitos. I thought about whether I could add a front porch or a covered back patio.

My house has an upstairs, which I visit as infrequently as possible. I bought the house knowing that my needs can all be met on the first floor, leaving the upstairs for my son to use so long as he lives with me. After that, as I age, I might get a university student to live for free with me, just to have someone in the house. But for that purpose, a separate entrance directly to the upstairs would be useful. I wondered about how to reconfigure the existing doorways and halls so as to construct a separate entrance.

My house has a small office, but really I need a bigger office. I have too many books, too many files, too many diplomas and awards and other work-related items. While I was working, I kept those diplomas and awards and files in my work office. Now, they sit in boxes in closets. With a bigger office, I could display my awards and my helicopter rotor-clock (a tale for another book) and other cool mementos I gathered over my Foreign Service years. I thought about how I could add on to my house so as to have a bigger office.

Besides thinking about the house, I thought about getting home and hosting a big Spanish dinner. I thought about who I would invite to the dinner and what food and wine I would serve. I thought about how I would decorate the table and what stories I would tell about the Camino.

I also thought—worried—a lot about my son. But I have done that ever since he came into my life. It was nothing new, nothing attributable to my time on the Camino.

As I neared the end of my Camino, I began to fret about not having had any Deep Thoughts. I tried convincing myself that there was a positive reason for that. Many pilgrims report going back over an old hurt or problem and finally reaching a resolution, or at least coming to peace with the problem. For a surprising number, that hurt involved a family member somehow taking advantage of them, either sexually or emotionally, when they were young. Or for others, it was monetary or work difficulties.

I decided I could be positive about not having Deep Thoughts because, when I have an issue or a problem, I try to confront it, and fix it, as soon as I can. If something is bothering me, it keeps me awake at night until I do something about it, even when I am reluctant to take action. I am unable to compartmentalize or bury the issue. The end result is that I have more or less dealt with the various traumas I have suffered over my thankfully long life, and I don't need to think deeply about them anymore. Or so I told myself.

When I got home, I laughingly told people that, clearly, I am a shallow person, because my deepest thoughts concerned remodeling my house and giving a welcome home dinner party. But I spoke too soon.

As I write this, a year after my long walk, I finally think I have parsed out the meaning of the Way for me.

In an earlier chapter, I recounted the story of The Almond Man. My meeting with him on the Meseta was just one example of the unexpected, unusual kindnesses that ordinary Spaniards regularly bestow on the strange foreign travelers in their midst. Spontaneously, without any hope of recompense of any kind, except of course perhaps in heaven, everyday Spaniards extend help to the pilgrims who flood their country. And this has been happening since the Camino began in the 800s. Many saints of the Middle Ages achieved their sainthoods by offering help and comfort to passing pilgrims.

I still marvel at The Almond Man, who was willing to stand under that broiling sun for hours, just to pass out a handful of almonds to passersby.

These sorts of occurrences are the intercultural currency of Camino gossip. Over dinner, we would ask new acquaintances, "Did you run into The Almond Man? What did he give you? Anything besides almonds?" My tinfoil-wrapped chocolate became a badge of honor.

On another occasion, we passed a house where a party in progress had spilled out into the street. We were invited to join the party. We initially declined since we were anxious to press on to our daily destination, but the hosts practically begged us to join them. We stayed for a while for a chat and a cup of wine. The hosts explained that offering food and drink to passing pilgrims was an important part of making their parties a success.

Another time we gratefully took a seat in the shade of a big tree for a brief rest. As soon as the couple in the nearby house saw us, they began pressing offers of beverages and then food on us.

"Take a cold beer! It will revive you for the rest of your walk!" offered the husband.

"Thanks," I replied, "but I'll curl up and go to sleep in this marvelous shade if I drink a beer."

"Well, how about a sandwich? I'm sure you are hungry," said the wife.

And on and on the offers rolled, from two elderly folks that I could see had little to spare. Despite their limited means, they were willing to share what they had with us. Like St. Martin of Tours, a favorite saint of the Middle Ages Camino pilgrims, they were willing to share everything with us, down to splitting their cloaks in half.

These small acts of kindness happened all along our Camino, and are a tribute to the bighearted character of Spaniards of all ages and socioeconomic groups.

I was thinking of this recently, as I listened to a story on NPR about a man in France who provides free lodging in his apartment to "illegal" refugees from the Mideast. From the way the Frenchman described it, he is part of a modern-day Underground Railroad offering help, sometimes illegal help, to migrants. The NPR story highlighted the struggles of the refugees to get to their destinations, and once there, to carve out a better life than the one they left behind.

Then I saw part of a documentary about a Greek coast guard captain whose daily task was to rescue migrants, or, if necessary, to pick up their bodies, from the cruel seas off the Greek islands.

As I think of all those Europeans trying to help refugees, I am shamed by the seemingly Grinch-like "heart two sizes too small" of our own political leaders, who are allowing only a small number of Mideastern refugees annually to enter the United States. I can't help but wonder what I can and should do to repay those many kindnesses James and I received in Spain, such as by volunteering with refugees, who, like the pilgrims of the Middle Ages, embark on long and uncertain journeys with no guarantee of reaching their goal.

Perhaps such small kindnesses are the real purpose of the Camino: to give people the opportunity to offer and receive help from strangers, thus reaffirming the proposition that Rousseau, not Hobbes, was correct about the essential goodness of humanity. I guess I have had my Deep Thoughts after all, though it took perspective, world events, and a year to bubble up to the surface.

Chapter 27
A Celebratory Dinner

D EEP THOUGHTS do not come naturally to me. In college, I rarely sat around those late-night BS sessions during which the meaning of life, Kafka, Camus, and nuclear winter were favorite topics. Nothing changed for me on the Camino. In Chapter 26 on "Deep Thoughts," I described the sorts of not-deep-at-all thoughts that floated through my mind as I trudged along, up and down the hills and across the flat, hot Meseta of the Camino.

Not too long into my journey, I did begin one train of thought that I kept thinking about for the whole route. I started planning in my head a dinner party, aimed at all those folks back in Houston who had aided me as I planned my journey. I would hold this dinner party as soon as I possibly could, once I got back to Houston.

I began with the guest list. As was true for Sleeping Beauty's parents, I had to make sure that I invited the right guests and didn't leave out anyone important. My guest list had to be limited to twelve or, at an absolute maximum, fourteen. This fact was dictated by the size of my dining room.

I purchased my house in Houston in part because it had the sort of dining room that I desired. Throughout my career in the Foreign Service, I enjoyed entertaining at home. Some officers preferred taking their contacts out to a restaurant, but I always found that inviting your foreign counterparts into your home for a sit-down dinner at which laughter and gossip could lighten the probing for information worked better. And many times those counterparts became more than just colleagues; they became friends.

When I was looking for my retirement house, I knew that I wanted a house with a dining room. Unfortunately, it seems that holding dinner parties has gone out of fashion in the United States, so few houses have large dining rooms. The house I eventually purchased had an acceptable formal dining room into which I could fit my china cabinet, bar/buffet, dining table, and about ten chairs. Since I have a dining table to which four leaves can be added and which can comfortably seat as many as sixteen, I knew when I purchased the house that I was never going to be able to extend my table to its fullest possible length.

Along the Camino I thought about arranging the dinner party so as to have two separate tables, increasing the number of people I could invite. The problem with that arrangement is that the guests who are not seated in the dining room always feel like second-class guests, having been seated at the smaller of the tables. Besides, I wanted us all together, talking about the Camino. That means I could host a maximum of twelve. I could actually invite fourteen, in the expectation that a couple of the invitees would be out of town or otherwise unable to accept the invitation.

The person on the top of my mental wish list was my Camino mentor, Julia Wagener, who had met with me throughout the months leading up to the trip to share her knowledge about the Camino and to offer advice. She had been an invaluable resource. I would look forward to seeing her lovely, smiling face at my table.

Next on the list were the three leaders of the Houston chapter of APOC: Linda Shubert, Kathi White, and Jeff Stys. By putting the time and effort into running the Houston chapter, they had made it possible for me to connect with many others who had walked or planned to walk the Camino. Among other fairy godmother and godfather gifts, they assign mentors to prospective walkers, and were the reason Julia took me on as a mentee.

I wanted my friend Eric Olson at the table. Eric was the person who had told me the most about blogging and pointed me in the direction of the platform I used for my blog while on the Camino.

And I thought it would be fun to have a few of the folks who had followed my blog, posting comments and feedback. I added Rob Connor and Sue Jean White to my guest list.

That brought the guest list to nine, including James and me. I later thought of adding an acquaintance whom I had enjoyed talking to at APOC gatherings, Matt, who had also connected with James. So, ten guests—a perfect number for my dining room!

Next, I could think about food. This was a fun game, and continued throughout the walk. Trudging along, it was sometimes hard to think about anything else but food.

For the main course: paella, no question. Way back before I had even heard about the Camino, my mother frequently made a great paella for dinner parties. Everyone always loved it. Not getting her recipe for paella is one of the things I have regretted since her death. At the time of her death, we children divided up her effects, and each of the five of us took away one of her notecard file boxes stuffed with recipes. I chose last, and got the one with desserts. Only later did I think that I should have ransacked the five boxes to copy my favorite recipes, but on the day of the great division of her effects there was really no time for anything like that. On the Camino I thought about asking my brothers if perhaps one of them had gotten the box with the paella recipe, and if he (all my living siblings are brothers) would share it with me.

From my time living in Spain in the 1970s, I knew that paella comes in many regional varieties. Would I serve Paella Valenciana, which includes savory chicken and deliciously steamed seafood? Or Paella de Mariscos (shellfish)? Or what?

Whenever we had paella along the Way, I paid particular attention to its ingredients. Once I decided that our main course had to be paella, James and I sought out saffron—the spice that turns the rice in the paella yellow—whenever we saw a spice shop. Those tiny strands of saffron are incredibly expensive, and a surprisingly dark red—not yellow—color.

So, paella it had to be. Dessert was equally easy to choose. I have always loved flan (egg pudding), and no other dessert would do. Occasionally, for variety, I order *arroz con leche* (rice pudding), mainly because I like the cinnamon on top. But, for my taste buds, *arroz con leche* is a distant second in the favorite Spanish dessert competition.

That left a lot of room for further contemplation. What should we have for a starter? By the time that James and I were well into our walk, I realized that he liked fried calamari (squid) as much as I did. In Spain, it isn't the tough, rubbery dish one so often encounters in the United States, but a soft, meltingly delicious delicacy wrapped in a lightly fried exterior. We ordered it a lot. But I had never cooked fried squid. Was I up to the task? It is always a mistake, in my experience, to cook something for the first time for guests.

Maybe a nice gazpacho—cold tomato soup with vegetables— would be a better choice? I had made gazpacho before, and quite liked how it turned out. So, yes, gazpacho would be on the menu.

And of course, following the Spanish tradition of having cheese after dessert, we would have to have a nice Manchego available.

On to the liquid refreshments. Sangria for cocktails. Maybe try the white wine sangria that was new to me on the trip? I'd have to ponder that a lot. And a really full-bodied red Rioja wine to go with the main course? Maybe a Spanish *jerez* (sherry) with the dessert? And definitely my old favorite standby liqueur, Licor 43, after dinner. Plus, I'd introduce my guests to my new favorite, Pacharán, with its deep ruby tint and slightly licorice taste.

But what about having something with sardines, which are cooked fabulously in Spain? Or asparagus, which we had so often on the trip? Or chorizo (Spanish sausage)? Or ox-tail soup, a Spanish favorite? How would I work those delicious Spanish olives into my menu? (No olives, customarily served with beer in Spain, ever survived being placed in front of James and me.)

The options danced through my head each day, diverting my thoughts from the hard, stony ground under my feet. As I sampled food along the way, I was constantly adjusting my proposed menu, adding and subtracting courses.

I didn't neglect bringing back little gifts for my guests. I bought a number of necklaces with blue shell-shaped pendants for the ladies. No one who has walked the Camino can see a shell pattern without thinking of the Camino. Finding something for the gentlemen, as always, was more difficult. I browsed around a lot of curio and tourist shops and picked up a number of small items, suitable for carrying in a backpack—a notepad and pen with Camino symbols, a small penknife in Spain's national colors, a small leather coin purse that cleverly folds up in a uniquely Spanish way.

And table decorations. Mustn't forget them!

What about appropriate flowers?

Should I have Spanish music softly playing in the background? Or would that be a distraction?

And so the planning went on, day by day.

Once back in Houston, I did indeed organize my dinner party. It did not turn out as perfectly as I had planned it in my head. Some of the guests I had wanted to attend were unable to do so. By chance, after returning to Houston I ate at a seafood restaurant that served excellent fried calamari, so I cheated and ordered from that restaurant for our calamari course rather than trying to make it myself. And good Americans that they are, cognizant of the need to be careful with drinking and driving, none of my guests partook of the full range of Spanish alcoholic beverages that I had on hand ready to serve. (The day I tracked down *Pacharán* in Houston after I returned was a happy day.) I had to polish off, with minimal help from others, the pitcher of sangria that James had conjured up for us, and consequently I was feeling no pain by the end of the evening.

Along the whole of the Camino, the large scallop shell that the Houston chapter of APOC had presented to me many months earlier was affixed to my backpack. At the very end of this dinner party, it was my pleasure to present back to the chapter leaders a few special scallop shells that I had collected along the route. I had thought about donating back the shell that had been given to me, but in the end it was too powerful a talisman, and I kept it safe with me, on display, a secret symbol joining together all who know its meaning.

FINAL MENU FOR THE DINNER

APPETIZERS: OLIVES, MANCHEGO CHEESE   SANGRIA

STARTER: FRIED CALAMARI

SOUP: GAZPACHO

MAIN COURSE: PAELLA VALENCIANA   RIOJA WINE

DESSERT: FLAN

AFTER DESSERT: MANCHEGO CHEESE   LICOR 43
PACHARÁN
SPANISH BRANDY

Chapter 28
Reading and Resources Suggestions

I T HAS BEEN MY EXPERIENCE that there are two types of travelers—the planners and the spontaneous, "let's just go and find our way day-by-day" types. At times, I've been spontaneous and just picked up at the last minute and headed out the door for a long weekend, without planning. But in general, and especially for long trips, I am a planner. And by "planner," I mean, above all, a reader.

Once long ago, while I was still working, I had a use-it-or-lose-it situation coming up with what was called "home leave," which had to be taken in the United States. I decided that my husband and I should go out west, to a part of the country that I had never before visited. I started asking colleagues what they recommended, studying maps, and ordering and reading guidebooks. I ended up having a lot of fun planning our trip—where it would start, the route we would take, and what we would see along the way. For the big must-see destinations, like national parks, I booked ahead at lodges and other special hotels. For the other days, I left our overnight accommodations up to chance. I knew in which town I wanted to pass the night, but not in what lodging. We ended up staying in some fabulous, historic lodges, but also in some run-down motels, one of which had housed the cast of one of the John Wayne movies shot in Monument Valley.

My discovery for that trip was that the *planning* of the trip can be every bit as pleasurable as the actual *taking* of the trip. And ever since then, I have been a dedicated reader-planner of trips. Reading ahead about what you are going to see, or might see, helps you to figure out what you most want to see, and frees you from being glued to your guidebook once you are actually there.

Here are some of the books I read before I started off on the Camino. I also suggest a couple of groups you might want to join.

MUST HAVES

Brierley, John. *A Pilgrim's Guide to the Camino de Santiago: St. Jean - Roncesvalles - Santiago.*

This book is the indispensable travel guide for anyone walking the French route. I carried it in one of the pockets of my cargo pants every day, and took it out numerous times a day to read about the Camino and the places through which we were passing. It will help you plan your trip ahead of time; it divides the trip into convenient *stages*; and it gives you information about towns along the way, plus names and phone numbers for places to stay in each village and town. The elevation maps and town maps are very helpful.

Brierley, John. *Camino de Santiago Maps: St. Jean Pied de Port - Santiago de Compostela (Camino De Santiago Map Guides).*

This is an abbreviated version of the book above, with just the maps and accommodation information included in it. I also carried this slim volume in my pants pocket, and pulled it out whenever I just wanted to consult a map.

Every traveler along the French route will have one or both of the above books. They are by far the most common practical guides.

Highly Recommended

Michener, James. *Iberia.* Chapter XIII: "Santiago de Compostela."
  As you know from having read this book, I myself place *Iberia* in the must-read category. However, for modern pilgrims, there are a couple of disadvantages to the book, namely, that it is somewhat dated, particularly in that Michener spends a lot of time on the political question of what will happen in Spain after Franco. A second disadvantage for those walking the Camino is that it is not a guide for walkers, having just one chapter specifically on the Camino—but that chapter is highly interesting.
  For anyone with the time, I urge you to read all of *Iberia.* I know no other book that delves so completely and well into Spain and into the character and psychology of the Spanish people. You will come away from *Iberia* with a much better sense of what Spain is all about. As for the specific chapter on the Camino, it was that chapter that hooked me on wanting to travel the Camino de Santiago so many years ago.

Gitlitz, David M. and Linda Kay Davidson. *The Pilgrimage Road to Santiago: The Complete Cultural Handbook.*
  A great resource for those who want to learn more about cultural sites of all sorts.

Recommended

Steves, Rick. *Spain.*
  Rick Steves' guidebook is as good as any to modern-day Spain. If you spend any amount of time in any of the larger cities along the Camino—Burgos, León, Santiago de Compostela—you will want a more complete guidebook than the longer Brierley book. Also, if you take my recommendation and spend a few extra days in Madrid and Toledo, you will need a general guidebook for Spain.

—. *Spain.* Michelin Green Guide.

The Michelin guides are my old standbys, and I usually carry a copy of the green guide. Much of the same ground is covered as in the Rick Steves' guidebook, but I love the Michelin system of giving stars to the sites, which helps me figure out what to see when I am short on time.

—. *Camino de Santiago: St-Jean-Pied-de-Port* [to] *Santiago de Compostela.*

Another map guidebook. I especially appreciated the elevation maps in this book. It's small and lightweight and easy to carry.

Kelly, Gerald. *Camino de Santiago - Practical Preparation and Background.*

This is a good book to read when you are starting your preparations for the trip. It has lots of practical advice, and will introduce you to the lingo of the Camino before you set out.

OTHER

Here are a few books I read ahead of time, with some comments.

Wyman, Mary O'Hara. *Grandma's on the Camino: Reflections on a 48-Day Walking Pilgrimage to Santiago.*

This was one of the more interesting day-by-day accounts I read before setting off on my journey. The author wrote and sent home a postcard every day, and those postcards form a large part of the book, but she also adds parts of her journal.

Moore, Tim. *Travels with My Donkey: One Man and His Ass on a Pilgrimage to Santiago.*

This is one of the funniest books about the Camino. It will have you laughing out loud at times. Tim Moore definitely chose a more challenging way to travel the Camino. His family joins him towards the end of the trip, so the book also gives you a sense of what it is like to travel the Camino with children.

Bonville, William J. *A Traveler's Highway to Heaven: Exploring the History and Culture of Northern Spain on El Camino de Santiago.*
Another book for those interested in the culture of the Camino.

Llewellyn, Evan. *My Own Damn Camino: True Tales from the Road.*
He offers some interesting stories from his journey.

Adams, Christine. *A Sometime Pilgrim: (mis)Adventures Along the Camino del Norte.*
Of special interest to those who want to walk the Camino del Norte rather than the French route.

Smith, Kay. *60 and Solo on the Camino de Santiago de Compostela.*
For those of us who are older, reading Kay Smith's book can build confidence that yes, you *can* walk the Camino.

Teague, Alessa. *The Long Road Home: One Woman's True Story of Reclaiming Her Life Along the Camino de Santiago.*
One of many books about finding oneself along the Camino, resetting goals, having Deep Thoughts, and the like.

Christmas, Jane. *What the Psychic Told the Pilgrim: A Midlife Misadventure on the Camino.*
It was interesting to me how many folks (or at least writers) seem to seek out romance on the Camino. Read this book if that topic interests you.

Kelly, Gerald. *Walking Guide to the Camino de Santiago: History Culture Architecture.*
Another resource for those interested in seeing things along the way rather than just walking.

* * *

And here are a few books I picked up along the Way, because they covered a topic I found interesting. You can probably order them ahead of time, if you wish to do so, or collect them along the Camino like I did.

—. *Legends of the Camino de Santiago*. Los Cuadernos de Urogallo Ediciones, 2010.

A very small but interesting recounting of some Camino "legends," though some of it is more history than legend. The story of St. James, the field of the stars, the reason the scallop is the symbol of the Camino, St. James and the Virgin Mary, Charles the Great (Charlemagne)—those are just a few of the legends covered.

Torres Sevilla, Margarita, and Jose Miguel Ortega del Riol. *Kings of the Grail*.

For those like me who are fascinated with the whole legend and mystique of the Holy Grail, this is a great read. The authors trace the Grail through history and give their best estimation about what really happened (or didn't happen) to the Holy Grail.

Diez Martinez, Josefina, Emma Bayon Blanco, and Maria Sanchez Rodriguez. *León Cathedral: A Gothic Dream*.

I highly recommend that all pilgrims carve out extra time to spend in the cathedrals of Burgos, León, and Santiago de Compostela. You can take a tour, which will be interesting and informative, and I recommend that you do so. However, nothing beats going around these cathedrals slowly, alone, with a good guidebook, and stopping for a longer look when something is particularly beautiful or interesting to you.

Barral, Alejandro, and Ramon Yzquierdo. *Santiago Cathedral: A Guide to Its Art Treasures*.

OTHER RESOURCES

Join APOC. You will get a newsletter, a patch for your backpack, and a lot of good advice. If there is a chapter in a city near you, be sure to go to meetings and gatherings. This is great way to get the latest information from recently returned travelers.

I also recommend that you sign up for the Facebook page "Slow Strollers on the Camino." This is another great resource, one that I didn't discover until I had already returned from my trip.

Chapter 29
Epilogue

NEITHER MY CAMINO CELEBRATORY DINNER party nor my Camino journey turned out as I had expected. My dinner party did not live up to the imaginings I had whipped up while walking the Camino. Guests I very much wanted to attend were unavailable. I chickened out of trying to make at home the fried calamari I so loved. My guests did not partake of all the wonderful Spanish liqueurs I had so painstakingly gathered. The dinner was really lovely, with wonderful guests, good food, lively conversation. And yet, it wasn't the magical evening I had dreamed about.

The Camino did not bring me the spiritual high that so many have written about. I loved visiting the north of Spain for the first time, getting to see Burgos and León cathedrals, walking in the footsteps of so many millions of previous pilgrims. And yet, the whole Camino experience seemed more secular and less religious than I was expecting.

I am not trying to end this account of my Camino journey on a low note. Rather, I am saying that I relearned on this trip what I had learned so long ago, on an autumn night in Houston, when I stepped out of my dorm with one idea of how the evening was going to unwind, only to find myself confronted with a far different experience, a life-changing one.

I started planning for the Camino thinking I would be traveling alone, that I could do the trip as planned, that the trip would unfold like a yellow brick road before me. Instead, I didn't travel alone. The Camino itself had twists and turns, unanticipated ups and downs, and a different pace than I expected. I won't characterize these changes as either good or bad—they just *were*. Man proposes, God disposes, as the saying goes. Or in this case, Woman plans, the Camino cans those plans and instead offers something different, unexpected, not religious or magical or mystical but still an experience like no other, a stream that stepped in will never be the same for any other pilgrim, or even for oneself at another time.

My Camino adventure, more than forty years in the planning, comes to an end as I publish this book.

ACKNOWLEDGMENTS

F IRST, I WOULD LIKE TO THANK all of the members of my two writing groups. My colleagues in Houston Writers Group - At Rice Village and Write Club: Houston listened to these chapters as I laboriously produced them one by one. They offered great advice, from the very first meeting at which I presented a chapter. In particular, I would like to thank Andrea (Andi) Keist and Danielle Husband for coordinating these groups. I needed deadlines, and these two groups gave them to me.

Second, I would like to thank the Houston chapter of APOC. The advice I received about the Camino was invaluable, and I still try to attend APOC meetings whenever I can to give back to those thinking about tackling the Camino. The three organizers of the Houston chapter during the lead up to my Camino trip, Kathi White, Linda Shubert, and Jeff Stys, deserve a particular shout-out for all of the love and dedication they pour into the local chapter. Jeff has now moved up to the APOC national board, and David Eickhoff has joined Kathi and Linda in managing the Houston chapter of APOC.

One of the best things I got from APOC was my mentor, Julia Wagener. Julia was a source of wonderful advice and constant encouragement, and I consider her a dear friend. I hope she and I can travel the Camino together some day.

With an exception or two that are noted, the author of this book or her son took all the photographs.

I wish to acknowledge my son, James A. Connor. James made my Camino so different from what I had planned, yet so important in a different way. As you will have read in the book, James saved my bacon on more than one occasion on the Camino—from the very first day on through some very tough days. His never-give-up attitude kept me going on some difficult slopes when I was ready to concede defeat and just sit down and bawl. He hopes to walk the Camino again in the future, and I hope that for him too.

My friend Eric Olson made this book possible through his careful editing, interior design, and technological know-how. Without Eric, this book might not have been published at all, and certainly not in the excellent form it has finally taken.

Xavier Comas came up with the wonderful cover design for the book. I believe it captures the essence of the book, that walking the Camino is great but is not the only way to experience the many fascinating facets of Spain and the Camino.

Mary Connor was pressed into service at the last minute to produce the delightful map illustrations that grace Chapter 23 of the book. Thanks, Mary, for friendship and assistance way beyond what I could have expected.

Also rendering last-minute help was Bayou City Press Staff Photographer Robert Connor, who gave advice about and assistance with the photographs you see in this book.

Without all of these wonderful folks, I would not have been able to build this homage to the Camino, which was accomplished not brick by brick but word by word and picture by picture.

Julie Gianelloni Connor
Houston, November 2019

INDEX OF PLACES, PEOPLE AND ORGANIZATIONS

ABOUT THE AUTHOR

I N WRITING THIS BOOK, Julie Gianelloni Connor is returning to her roots as someone who grew up surrounded by books. Born and raised outside of Baton Rouge, Louisiana, Julie grew up as a country girl. She was the only female among a gang of neighborhood boys, playing football and baseball with them, riding horses, and most of all reading. She devoured books, and patronized the nearest bookmobile whenever she could. Nancy Drew mysteries were early favorites, as were any books she could get her hands on about horses.

For her last two years of high school, Julie was sent to the Dana Hall School in Wellesley, Massachusetts, where her step-grandmother had studied as a girl. This was her first experience in the wider world, and it occurred during a turbulent time in the United States. She headed back south for college, attending Rice University in Houston, where she majored in English and history.

As she recounts in this book, her studies were interrupted in the fall of her junior year when she was the victim of violent crime, which led her to drop out of Rice University and go to Europe. In Lisbon she received a certificate in Teaching English as a Foreign Language and spent the next two years teaching English, first in Lisbon and then in Barcelona and London. Those early years in Europe ignited Julie's love of travel.

After returning to the United States, Julie completed her undergraduate degree at Rice University and then entered the master's degree creative writing program at the University of Houston, where she worked as a teaching fellow instructing freshman and sophomores in writing and literature. Marriage and a variety of jobs followed. In 1981, Julie was invited to join the U.S. Foreign Service and departed Houston for Washington, DC.

Over a 33-year diplomatic career, Julie served her country overseas in Tel Aviv, Israel (twice); Asunción, Paraguay; Guatemala City, Guatemala; Jakarta, Indonesia; Bogotá, Colombia (twice); Kuala Lumpur, Malaysia; and Santiago, Chile. While assigned to Washington, she served in fields as diverse as nuclear nonproliferation, arms control, and women's issues. During her diplomatic years, she was assigned to the National War College, earning a master of science degree in National Security Strategy. Her last assignment for the Foreign Service was as the Diplomat in Residence at the University of Texas in Austin, where she taught diplomacy at the LBJ School of Public Affairs. Her career was filled with writing, but it was writing in the form of memoranda, briefing notes, and reports back to Washington for government readers.

After retirement from the Foreign Service, Julie returned to Houston. Her first post-retirement long trip was to walk the Camino de Santiago in Spain, the story of which is recounted in this book.

Readers can learn more about Julie by visiting her website, JulieConnorAuthor.com. There, you are encouraged to sign up for her newsletter. You can also follow her on Facebook (Facebook.com/JulieGianelloniConnorAuthor) and LinkedIn (Linkedin.com/in/Julie-Gianelloni-Connor-87b97328).

Bayou City Press
THE WORLD IN PRINT

ABOUT BAYOU CITY PRESS

IN ITS FIRST YEAR OF OPERATION, Bayou City Press, located in Houston, Texas, has concentrated on establishing a firm foundation in the community. Founder/editor Julie Gianelloni Connor has joined the Houston writing and publishing scene, attending meetings of writing groups and writing organizations. Julie is a member of the Houston Writers Guild, the Houston chapter of the Nonfiction Authors Association, and the Houston Independent Authors Group, as well as two critique groups.

Bayou City Press has three areas of concentration: travel writing, writing about Houston, and writing on international affairs.

Bayou City Press launched its website in May 2019, showcasing columns penned by Houston authors about foreign travel. Joining Julie Connor as travel writers were contributors Andi Keist and Mary Connor. Columnist Stephanie McCall-McLendon contributed articles about Houston and charity-related events in the Houston area. As the year proceeded, additional contributors Dennis Carnes and Shay Hill published on the website. You can read these authors' columns at BayouCityPress.com.

In the autumn of 2019, Bayou City Press began new activities by sponsoring an International Travel Book Club and an International Film Club. These groups meet to evaluate and discuss books and films with overseas settings.

In October 2019, Bayou City Press threw open the doors of its new offices for the official launch of the company.

Bayou City Press plans to add column contributors, publish additional book titles, and begin carrying fiction as well as non-fiction. While Bayou City Press maintains a focus on travel, Houston, and international affairs, we invite book-length submissions on any topic for consideration. Submit letters of inquiry to the following address:

Bayou City Press
10303 Scofield Lane
Houston, TX 77096

Bayou City Press welcomes short pieces (approximately 1,000–3,000 words) for its online columns. Please submit questions about short articles via the website, BayouCityPress.com.

Help the Author

Solve Mysteries

Did you walk the Camino in 2016? I'd love your help in identifying some of the people I met along the Camino: the New Jersey Six, the two couples from Louisiana, Randy from Miami, and Veronica from Romania. If you can offer information about these or other people and places mentioned in this book, please email me at Julie@BayouCityPress.com. I will update the forthcoming eBook version accordingly and acknowledge your contribution on my blog.

Write Reviews

If you enjoyed reading this book, please help me and other readers by writing a review on Amazon.com and elsewhere. What you think about this book matters to me and others. Please share your feedback. The Camino community is global, and others in distant places will appreciate your reaction to *Savoring the Camino de Santiago*.

Visit My Website and Blog
Sign Up for My Newsletter

I invite you to visit my website at JulieConnorAuthor.com. There, you can sign up for my Bayou City Press Newsletter. I also invite you to visit my blog at CaminoforBoomers.com. My blog features color photos about this pilgrimage, including color versions of the photos printed in this book. On the blog you can also read updates about my correspondence with the Government of Spain concerning the Camino, as well as other relevant information pertaining to this book.

Made in the USA
Las Vegas, NV
16 January 2022

41577223R00153